"[*Hanging Out*] is exploring this downstream consequence of isolation, of loneliness, of atomization, which I think is pretty underexplored."

—EZRA KLEIN

"*Hanging Out* is rich with illuminating stories with [a] surprising vibe, from a hair-raising tale of a wild night spent with a group of strangers in Scotland to a bridge-burning chronicle of the university chancellor who stuck her with a $200 tab. It reads like a book written by someone who goes out intending to make some new memories as often as possible, and then saves them up for the perfect moment to retell them. Real hanging out, Liming writes, is *about* stories, indeed consists mostly *of* stories ... I passionately believ[ed] that her book was *right.*"—DAN KOIS, *SLATE*

"From sharing a cuppa to lazing in the park, is the key to happiness doing everyday activities with pals? . . . Liming proposes hanging out as a balm that forges connection and meaning." —*THE GUARDIAN UK*

"We could all use more of that blissfully unstructured social time, posits Sheila Liming in the well-considered series of arguments found in *Hanging Out.*" —*READER'S DIGEST*

"[*Hanging Out*] opens with a simple and expansive account of what hanging out is . . . Liming dedicates much of the book to stories from her past. She has lived an interesting life, and she tells these stories well."

—*WASHINGTON POST*

"More books about hanging out, less about productivity please. Sheila Liming sees the gap in our thinking about time, and the true worth in spending it in an unstructured fashion with members of our community."

—*LITERARY HUB*

"[*Hanging Out*] encourages readers to do more of it in real life . . . Liming's observational and storytelling skills shine." —**PUBLISHERS WEEKLY**

"A thoughtful manifesto ... Liming is unsurprisingly the most compelling when she incorporates literary criticism into her treatise."

—**BOOKPAGE**

"Tightly argued, brilliantly written ... smart yet so accessible, *Hanging Out* will impress readers with the way each idea builds on the next, never forced and always human."   —**SHELF AWARENESS**

"Readers will gain a new appreciation for their next get-together after reading this fascinating book and taking the author's well-written words to heart."   —**BOOKLIST**

"[A] meditation on the value of spending idle time with friends, family, and strangers."   —**KIRKUS REVIEWS**

"While Liming does champion traditional forms of sociability, she is not some idealized social butterfly determined to Emily Post us all into the perfect soirée attendees. She writes of parties that sound exhausting, of dinner-party guests who still owe her money, and even of attending a party and realizing that the host didn't like her."

—**SEVEN DAYS**

"Informed by her own experiences and anecdotes—chiefly from moving across the United States during the pandemic—Liming also brings a rich knowledge of pop culture and intellectual history to persuasive arguments about the importance of spending casual and unproductive time with other people."   —**ZOOMER MAGAZINE**

HANGING OUT

THE RADICAL POWER OF KILLING TIME

Sheila Liming

MELVILLE HOUSE
BROOKLYN • LONDON

HANGING OUT: THE RADICAL POWER OF KILLING TIME

First published in 2023 by Melville House
Copyright © Sheila Liming, 2022
All rights reserved.
First Melville House Printing: November 2022

Melville House Publishing
46 John Street
Brooklyn, NY 11201
and
Melville House UK
Suite 2000
16/18 Woodford Road
London E7 0HA

mhpbooks.com
@melvillehouse

ISBN: 978-1-68589-078-0
ISBN: 978-1-68589-006-3 (eBook)

Library of Congress Control Number: 2022946367

Designed by Beste M. Doğan

Printed in the United States of America
10 9 8 7 6 5 4 3 2 1

A catalog record for this book is available from the Library of Congress

For Dave,

my favorite person to hang out with.

INTRODUCTION

I was looking at a field of sunflowers. They were dead—black, desiccated, their honeycombed faces having been pecked or otherwise stripped of their former multitudes of seeds. They looked stranded to me, caught between the season of their flourishing and the next one, the one that would see them all plowed under.

"Nothing gold can stay," I commented with a quick nudge to my partner, Dave, who was beside me in the passenger seat.

We were on our way to Sherry and Virgil's house and taking our chances with detours because we had extra time. A strip of dirt road divided the field of dead sunflowers from Old Crossing and Treaty Park, which is a sort of wayside stopping point along the Red Lake River, in western Minnesota. Every time we saw Sherry and Virgil, they would tell us to visit the park and read about the oxcarts that, back in the mid-1800s, used to cross there on their four-hundred-plus-mile journeys from Winnipeg to St. Paul. The spot was one of the only of its kind along the river, shallow and wide enough to allow the oxen to get across. This made it an important place in an otherwise unimportant landscape: nearby Red Lake Falls, the town where Sherry and Virgil lived, had recently been named the "worst place to live in America" by a *Washington Post* reporter who used data, apparently, to justify that ranking.[1]

Dave and I had driven over that morning from our home in Grand Forks, which sits about thirty miles west, right where the Minnesota border cozies up to its neighbor, North Dakota. It was Sherry who had invited us, luring us with promises of late-season produce—squash and potatoes and pumpkins from the fields that she and Virgil tended together on their land, apples from their trees, late-season raspberries that could still be found clinging to their bushes. We had to stop off on the way to pick up a piece of used furniture, an oak cabinet we had bought off of Craigslist. We had it behind us in the back, swaddled in wool blankets that were moth-pocked and no good to us anymore, when we paused at the park and stepped out of the car.

Winter had done its thing already and blanched our surroundings, though it was only October. As we examined the plaques that explained about the oxcarts (and also about the treaty that had forced the Red Lake band of Chippewa to cede the fertile farmlands of Red River Valley to the U.S. government), a few flakes of snow slipped down, let loose from a sky that was as gray as the grass. Across the road, all those charred-looking sunflowers clicked and creaked in the wind.

We didn't stay long; it was too cold. But it gave us a chance to pause and issue some advanced warning to our hosts.

Dave made the call and it was Virgil who answered. "We'll be there in about twenty minutes," he said, explaining the part about the stop in Crookston and the oak cabinet.

"Twenty minutes? Great! I'll get lunch started."

I could hear Virgil's voice loud and clear through the phone. He had a habit of shouting because, now in his seventies, he was getting to be hard of hearing. Virgil and Sherry always had lunch to offer, no matter what time of day it was, and it was always a good lunch: venison stew, baked squash with wild rice, hot raspberries poured over vanilla ice cream for dessert. Their life on the farm always struck me as being one of plenty, no matter what the guy from *The Washington Post* had to say about it. They had sheep and alpacas and an old donkey, who was partial to being fed carrots and receiving pets on the nose, plus chickens and cats, and dogs running circles around the chickens and cats. Though my partner and I saw them every day in the halls at the university where we worked, we were always happy to haul out to Minnesota on the weekends to hang out with Sherry and Virgil at their home.

"Okay, see you soon," said Dave, and he was in the process of hanging up when we both heard Virgil's voice again.

"Hang on—" Dave put the phone back up to his ear.

"What's that, Virgil?"

"I'm sorry . . . what did you say your name was?"

Virgil had missed the part at the beginning of the call when Dave had identified himself. "It's Dave . . . as in Dave and Sheila? We work together?"

"Oh, oh, *great!*" Virgil seemed even more excited now that he knew who it was that he was making lunch for. Dave hung up the phone and we sat there for a second and watched the flakes land and grow runny there on the windshield.

"We could have been strangers off the street and he would still be making us lunch," Dave said. He shook his head and smiled in charmed disbelief.

Hanging out is about daring to do nothing much and, even more than that, about daring to do it in the company of others. The concept of hanging out covers a broad spectrum of activities—some of them accidental and improvisational, some of them rather structured and planned (as in the kind of hanging out that happens at a formal gathering like a wedding, say). Regardless of the specific occasion, though, or of the amount of planning that has gone into creating it, the objective is the same: it's about blocking out time and dedicating it to the work of interacting with other people, whoever they might be.

In the case of my old colleague, Virgil, it didn't matter who we were. Dave was right: we could have been strangers—anybody with access to his phone number—and he would have been just as interested in our story about procuring the oak cabinet and in the prospect of hanging out with us over lunch. But what impressed me most in this instance was how quickly and easily that response took shape in him, like it wasn't a choice so much as a reflex or a built-in feature. Virgil was *down to hang out*; what's more, his inclination and willingness to do so superseded, even, his interest in finding out who it was that he was supposed to be hanging out with. Sherry must have forgotten to tell him that we were coming, or else he forgot that she had told him, and yet the news of receiving unexpected company didn't appear to bother him in the slightest.

As bemused as I was by Virgil's enthusiasm, I found my own reaction to it even more perplexing. Why, I wondered, did this not feel normal? Why, and through what means, had my expectations been engineered to prepare me for a different kind of scenario, one in which having strangers show up at your house for lunch might be viewed as an unwelcome incursion, as an inconvenience? Why did hanging out feel so hard at times if, in reality, it could be that easy? What forces prevented it from feeling that way all the time?

The story I've been telling about visiting Sherry and Virgil at their home took place several years ago and, since then, a lot has changed. For instance, I don't live in North Dakota anymore. When I hang out with Sherry and Virgil now, I'm forced to do it via email or video chat or phone, or else through the occasional letter or Christmas card. This is not the same as having lunch with them, in the little, three-room house that they built themselves and installed on the land that Virgil inherited from his parents, around the low table made from a single, crosscut slab of polished wood. It's not the same, but it is, in its own way, more customary, since it bears resemblance to the methods that govern much of the hanging out I do these days. Digital devices and technologies make that other kind of hanging out easier, but they also strip it of the experiences and particularities of place. What gets lost, along with those particularities, are deeper shades of connection, intimacy, and meaning.

I'm interested in what it means to forge those very things— connection, intimacy, and meaning—in a world that feels increasingly hostile to all three. This is a world, by the way, that started to take shape long before the average person ever learned the word "coronavirus." Indeed, the conditions of this world have been forming for decades in response to an intricate combination of pressures: the expansion of digital technologies and our increasing reliance on them; the growth of the private sector and accompanying diminishment of the public sphere; policies and social practices that champion individualism and make social connection more difficult; and an ethos of do-it-yourself ruggedness that has taken the place of shared support structures. The coronavirus pandemic made all of these things worse and perhaps more visible to the naked eye, but it did not invent them. We were having a hard time hanging out well before COVID-19 came along and made hanging out hard.

For the past few decades, we humans have been adjusting and varying our approaches to hanging out in light of the growth of technologies that make doing so in person, if not unnecessary, more or less optional. Much of that hanging out has been happening on the internet, even while some of it has continued to take place in person. But COVID tipped the balance, marking the moment that hanging out went from being primarily about in-person activity to being primarily about internet-based activity. Where we once turned to digital devices to supplement whatever we did in person while hanging out, now it's the reverse: hanging out, for an increasing majority of us, begins with those digital devices and only occasionally occurs without their aid. For some people, especially young people, this was likely already true, back before the pandemic; now, though, it's a truth that seeps forth with the potency of an oil spill, covering over everything and everyone.

There are good reasons to question, to interrogate, and to resist the shift toward a life lived online. One of them involves preserving the separation between work and leisure, since hanging out online looks a lot like hanging out at work. Writer Amelia Horgan observes, "As work extends over more and more of human social life . . . , possible countervailing forms of recognition—from friendship, from our hobbies, from shared social practices—dissolve."[2] Along with that dissolution comes the mutation of basic social interactions, which start to resemble the kind we are forced to perform at work. In both cases, relational connections get distilled and reduced to the raw functionality of information exchange. We send text messages back and forth, gleaning basic knowledge from them, but we do not hear the other person's breath, clock the fluctuations in their vocal register, or notice the way that emotions tug at the edges of an otherwise composed facial expression. We are not there next to them in order to do any of this, nor are we there to offer physical reassurance when all those emotions start to pile up, to feel a little too heavy and burdensome. We can send an emoji, which is a virtual substitute for the physical expression of emotion, but we cannot offer the other person the simple gift of our physical attention, awareness, or touch. We cannot embrace them.

The Italian philosopher Antonio Gramsci spent more than ten years in prison, from 1926 until his death in April of 1937. His crime was protesting against fascism through his activism and writing, deeds that, under emergency legislation following the attempted assassination of the fascist dictator Benito Mussolini, were made illegal in Italy. Gramsci died in prison and, about a decade afterward, became posthumously famous through the publication of his celebrated *Prison Notebooks*, which combine essays on political theory with historical analysis and criticism of the carceral state. He wrote the *Prison Notebooks* while he was being held captive, and during that time, he also wrote letters. The majority of those letters were written to a woman named Tania, who was his wife's sister and something of a familial ambassador to him in prison. In his letters to Tania, Gramsci describes his longing to be near his family members, including his two young sons, about whom he hungered for details. And in most of them, he employs a version of a standard sign-off: "I embrace you." He uses this language of physical embrasure even when the correspondent is a friend, a fellow intellectual, or a political ally, adopting it to say things like, "I embrace you fraternally, together with all our friends."[3]

It was one of my own friends, Carleton, who first alerted me to this rhetorical flourish of Gramsci's. The phrase "I embrace you," in my friend's view, seems to symbolize Gramsci's appetite for physical closeness and proximity. It gestures toward a spectrum of wished-for tenderness. Gramsci's hypothetical embraces range from familial to intimate (as when addressing a letter to his wife) to genial to warmly professional. At the time when my friend pointed this out to me, I had recently moved to North Dakota and he and I were sending physical letters back and forth. We both ended up adopting Gramsci's "I embrace you" as a way of bridging the space between us, of shrinking it down into something that felt more manageable—a mere arm's length, maybe. At the same time, the means that we were using to communicate, by which I mean physical letters sent through the mail, served to remind us of the realities of that distance. It forced us to feel what text messages and FaceTime could not: the fact of our separation, which had been wrought by our commitments to certain, physical places.

One reason to fight for the right to hang out, then, begins with an awareness of the potential that digital technologies and devices possess to obscure the realities of place. This is an idea that the artist and writer Jenny Odell develops in her book *How to Do Nothing*. In it, Odell investigates the merits of what she calls "placefulness," which stands opposed to "the placelessness of an optimized life spent online."[4] Through an extension of Odell's observations, it becomes possible to see placelessness as a primary means by which digital technology seeks to convert all time into work time. Rebecca Solnit was observing that very conversion more than twenty years ago, back in 2000, when she wrote, "The multiplication of technologies in the name of efficiency is actually eradicating free time by making it possible to maximize the time and place for production and minimize the unstructured traveled time in between." In her book *Wanderlust*, Solnit links the erosion of time spent doing one of the most basic of human activities, walking, to conditions of "false urgency" that preach that "travel is less important than arrival."[5] The same, I think, is true of hanging out, which, like walking, is so basic a pursuit that it is liable to get taken for granted. But what gets taken for granted also becomes an easy candidate for eradication. An insistence on hanging out, and especially on hanging out in person, serves to enforce divisions between work and leisure; it marks the boundaries of a sanctuary space that exists at a remove from the pressures of market-driven competition.

It also helps to combat what has been deemed an epidemic of loneliness. This is the phrase that Vivek H. Murthy, a former U.S. surgeon general, uses to describe one of the most pernicious and yet neglected health issues facing the modern world. Citing research conducted within the field of neuroscience, Murthy explains that the human body, bred to function as a social animal, "read[s] isolation, and often even the threat of isolation, as emergency."[6] What results is a state of "hypervigilance" that is designed to operate with one goal in mind: self-preservation. Murthy documents how our humanoid ancestors used such hypervigilance to their advantage when faced with the threat of isolation, which, to them, meant danger: "The whole body was engaged in self-preservation, narrowing attention to immediate signals, ignoring more leisurely thoughts, such as desire or wonder or reflection, and keeping sleep shallow and fragmented, lest a predator attack in the night."[7] That is to say, the type of nervous hypervigilance inspired by isolation, or even by the mere prospect of isolation, has historically resulted in antisocial responses and tendencies in humans, including the inability to experience or share feelings of desire or delight.

My own intellectual training has taught me to look askance at these kinds of studies, the kind that rely on essential claims about what all humans beings do or are like—the kind that inspire the sort of lazy causality to be found in statements like "since the dawn of time." Insisting that "our ancestors," itself a specious phrase, did x or y is, too often, an invitation to dangerous and highly generalized thinking. But I'm also drawn to some of Murthy's findings about how the human body responds to social stimuli or, in this case, to the absence of it. A student of mine, an absolute powerhouse of a writer named Amy, once wrote about the experience of falling asleep during a party. She explained in her essay that she doesn't usually sleep well but that, upon taking a two-hour nap in a friend's attic while a party was happening downstairs, she experienced the best sleep of her life. Over the past year or so since I read this, I've continued to think about what it means to rest feeling enfolded in social activity, even if one does not find themselves at the center of it. This thought brings to mind some of Murthy's points about how the human nervous system careens into overdrive when faced with isolating circumstances. Amy's story, meanwhile, illustrates the reverse and shows how a person can come to know the serenity of effortless inclusion when given mere proximity to certain, affirming forms of social experience.

Given its power as a healing venture, then, what I'm calling for in this book is more hanging out: more parties, more shared meals, more in-person gatherings, more late-night conversations, more being together in public, more cooperation, more standing shoulder to shoulder, more social revelry. This might sound like a call for a *return* to hanging out, but I'm conscious of the futility of viewing it in this way—of returning to anything or anywhere. This is not a *make hanging out great again* manifesto, but rather a call to remember what it was that we used to do and why we used to do it as a means of subjecting our social muscles to more rigorous and well-rounded training now, today. The point of that training is to prepare us for a more socially enhanced, as opposed to socially divided, future. I've styled this conversation as a tour of the many ways in which hanging out happens in contemporary culture—at dinner parties, on the job, on TV, on the internet. My task, as I have tried to see it, has been to supply commentary and, where it's deserved, criticism about the meaning of each. But I've worked to position myself less as an expert or authority on the subject and more as something of a docent, or a zealously informed volunteer. I don't want to lecture; rather, I want to take readers through this little gallery I've arranged containing portraits of accidents in modern living; I want to walk and talk with them; I want us all to hang out.

This book, then, is partly a manifesto and partly an invitation to come meander. The manifesto part is important; it's the insistent soundtrack to all that meandering, one that never quite fades or dies out. Its purpose is to ensure that the end of this, our walk together, doesn't come as an end, but rather as an incitement to continuation and new, increasingly bold applications. The manifesto part seeks to take what gets talked about here and make it manifest, or tangible, or real. The author Zadie Smith, commenting on what she sees as the inherent anti-timeliness of manifestos, warns against investing such writing with too much urgency. "Even when artists write manifestos, they are (hopefully) aware that their exigent tone is, finally, borrowed, only echoing and mimicking the urgency of the guerilla's demands, or the activist's protests, rather than truly enacting it."[8] What she's saying is that manifestos, as a genre, aspire to an impossible kind of exigence. They conjure feelings of immediacy that cannot be borne out since, by nature, any published manifesto is doomed to make a delayed entrance upon the scene of the conversation that inspired it. But in the case of hanging out, I can take some comfort in the fact that the conversation is a long one. It's been going on for some time already and shows no signs of ceasing, though the means of communicating and entering into it have shifted and may well continue to do so.

This book is partially about me but, to an even greater and more significant extent, it is about the larger world that I inhabit. I am speaking, in an ecosystemic sense, of a world of other people, other voices, other stories, and other books. I cannot write without these other influences by my side, urging me on; but what's more, I cannot, in an ethical sense, imagine a world in which writing without them would be viewed as acceptable or permissible. Insofar as hanging out describes a process that unfolds in group settings and so is necessarily shared, writing, for me, constitutes a kind of hanging out with the ideas and books and writers, both living and dead, who have shaped my thinking. My writing and stories do not belong solely to me but to the whole social universe that was the compound site of their creation. I have never done anything by myself—not truly, even when I was alone or felt certain that I *was* by myself. Writing, though it would appear to grow from the experience of solitary reflection, is no exception, not if it's done right.

My goal in writing this book has been to create a conversation around the subject of hanging out, one that clears a space for the serious consideration of how such a simple act became so incredibly hard for many of us, and what might be done to dismantle some of the pressures and obstacles that persist in making it that way. For instance, one of the biggest hindrances to hanging out, as I argue throughout the book, is rooted not just in the demands of work but in the blind drive toward ceaseless productivity, even when "work," in a formal sense, is not even supposed to be part of the equation. In a production-obsessed society, complaints *against* hanging out are often framed in racist or classist terms: we are suspicious of those who hang out when they ought to be working and producing, or suspicious of activities that do not resemble our personal understandings of work. We look askance at the people who engage in them; we pass laws designed to inhibit their abilities to congregate and evade work; we banish them and tell them to take their hanging out elsewhere—to the worst parts of our cities, to private spaces that quarantine them and the whole, generalized infection of idleness.

But this view of hanging out obscures the creative nature of indolence: creativity takes thought and thought takes time. What I'm arguing for here, then, is the reclaiming of time, which is both the essence of hanging out and its main ingredient, along with the reclaiming of the basic material components that are required for the so-called killing of time, by which I mean space. When we set aside time and space for hanging out, we assert our right to be non-productive, in the economic sense, and likewise our right to produce *differently*, by focusing on the work that is required for the strengthening of social ties. Sacred to the radical character of hanging out is the fact that anyone can do it, so long as they have access to time and space. Yet, as I write this, space in America is at a premium. The real estate market has surged through the roof, the result of peoples' efforts to gobble up what little private space is left now that the majority of public space has been abandoned, privatized, made dangerous or unpleasant, or otherwise deemed off limits. Hanging out, then, centers on a series of acts of refusal, all of which stem from the initial refusal to retreat. But it also acknowledges that the act of retreat itself tends to be shackled to the quest for safety, or for protection from perceived threats. COVID made hanging out hazardous; even now, several years after the pandemic's onset, those hazards persist for many, which is why I insist on a wide terrain for the consideration of what hanging out means in this book. Hanging out, which is already hard, is only made harder, not to mention more unequal, if we neglect to take those hazards into account.

Like all manifestos, then, this one brims with utopian urges and visions, even as it endeavors to keep reality firmly in its sight. It invites readers to contemplate the attractions of a more ideal situation and to hold them up against the lived experiences of a less ideal one. It recruits them to join in the fight against the narrowing of all that experience. And instead of 280 characters, or whatever can be squashed onto a smartphone's screen, it offers a wide-angle view of what could be and should be and *can* be.

In exchange, it asks a few things of you, the reader, starting with this one: put your phone facedown on the table, the way you do when you're talking to a friend who really needs your attention. Or better yet, throw it out the window. Take off your coat. Pull up a chair. Grab yourself a beverage. Hang out for a bit.

HANGING OUT

1

HANGING OUT

AT PARTIES

This is a non-Facebook party.

This is what it says on the back of the invitation, which is a paper invitation, and which I probably received some time during the spring of 2005. A long time ago, in other words—a whole, other world ago.

This invitation came to me through my campus mailbox, back when that was how things worked, or at least how they worked for us at the small Ohio college where I was an undergraduate. Students at the College of Wooster were assigned to physical mailboxes located in the campus center. The boxes in question were old, though not as old as I liked to imagine them—they probably only dated from the 1950s or '60s —and made of decorative brass. The combinations for the preset locks never changed. If you graduated and then came back to visit, you could open up a stranger's mailbox by using the old sequence of letters and numbers to work the quaint little brass dials. And they were tiny, these boxes, capable of holding only a few letters or handwritten notes.

The notes got deposited through a slot on the door of the box. This system had its advantages: it allowed the note's author to bypass campus mail, and along with it, the prying eyes of student mail workers. In that way, they were like the direct messages (in contemporary social media parlance) of their time—private, targeted, intimate. Meanwhile, magazines and packages and anything of that sort had to be picked up separately, at the front desk. Which is why they aren't there anymore, the old brass mailboxes; which is why ones just like them are now sold as nostalgia objects on sites like eBay and Etsy.

Back then, we students used to check our mailboxes a dozen or so times each day—on our way to meals in the cafeteria, which was located upstairs, or between classes. From those little brass boxes came good news in the form of scholarship announcements, class schedules, and dean's list notifications, and also less good news in the form of tuition bills and academic probation warnings. Graduate program acceptances came to me through my own little brass box. So did rejections. So did notes from secret admirers. So did invitations to parties.

The students who threw those parties, and sometimes I was one of them, would make up print invitations, duplicate them on library Xerox machines, and then slip them through the slots on the front of those mailboxes. The invitations were whimsically crude little things, more like zines than formal missives, featuring cut-and-paste collage images, hand-drawn graphics, and announcements scrawled in Sharpie. For most parties, a print invitation wasn't necessary, but it was a way of knowing that, were you to show up, you might find yourself officially welcome.

I don't remember any of these parties. Which is to say, I remember all of them all at once, mashed together into a kaleidoscopic slurry of memory. But I don't retain impressions of what they meant as individual instances. That includes this particular party, the one mentioned on the print invitation in question, which I still have.

This is a non-Facebook party.

What did that phrase mean to us in 2005? That was the year that Facebook "broke" on our campus, as it did on so many others. It was also the year that Facebook "broke," in a different sense, our old methods of social interaction and started rewiring our expectations for collective ritual. And what, I can't help but wonder, does that phrase mean today, now that parties are more likely than not to be facilitated via sites like Facebook—to take place *on* sites like Facebook, even, maybe, via livestream technology?

My friends Joe and Ronny sent me this print invitation to a designated "non-Facebook" party that happened almost twenty years ago now. It started at 11 p.m., the invitation tells me, and took place, as all our parties did, in a dorm room. The "non-Facebook" part was meant as a reference to the manner in which invitations were to be distributed. Already in 2005, after less than a year of living with Facebook and its slowly tightening chokehold, we knew what was happening: we could smell the impending changes in the air. The phrase "non-Facebook" was a way of announcing that the party in question would be organized around the old social networks— people who were already friends, or friends-of-friends, and thus part of an existing web of affiliation, as opposed to a categorically generalized and algorithmically selected one.

This method was supposed to stand in contrast to other, newer kinds of parties, "Facebook parties." Invitations to them were distributed online via the social networking platform, usually to anyone and everyone who had a Facebook account linked to our college. This was back when Facebook accounts were still being offered exclusively to college-age populations and were therefore tied to users' institutions—back before our uncles and grandmothers joined the site, before coffee shops and pizza restaurants and bands and municipalities all had their own profiles. As a result, Facebook parties, back in 2005, constituted something of a paradox, viewed on the one hand as exclusive (because Facebook itself was still exclusive) and on the other as democratic (because for many of them, all you had to do to get invited was be on Facebook).

I wasn't on Facebook in 2005. Indeed, to this day, I've never been. So I didn't get invited to those other parties, the Facebook-friendly ones. But sometimes I tagged along with others who did and I remember witnessing the change, which was not slow and gradual but fast and feverish, actually. You could tell a Facebook party by the photos. The point was to post them to Facebook the next day so everyone could like and distribute and repost as needed. I think this may have felt, at first, like a way of keeping the party going. But it soon revealed itself as a form of vulgar promotion that, over time, started to feel less vulgar and simply habitual, instead. The party had to be advertised, both before and after it happened, and so did the attendees. One had to like and distribute and follow back in order to lay claim to a certain status as a person considered worthy of inclusion, even though the process by which one had been selected for inclusion was itself non-selective. It became a game, a race. People started to collect friends, experiences, and parties like trading cards, hoarding them away in their online personality silos. The parties themselves, they stopped being about having fun and started being primarily about *looking* like you were having fun— about advertising your own capacity to have fun.

I remember feeling uneasy about all of this. Friends who would have previously invited me to parties stopped inviting me, or rather they stopped thinking of me, because they were content to let Facebook do the thinking for them. The digital tool that was supposed to be expanding friend networks had actually started to unmake them. Some of my friends shared these feelings of uneasiness. So together, the group of us kept at it with our non-Facebook party invites and our lists of campus mailbox numbers, and we folded and stuffed those print invitations through the front slots of those old brass mailboxes, and we made cute little appetizers to serve at our parties, where we counted on knowing the names of the majority of the people who might walk through the door.

We busied ourselves with the building of these paper barricades. We knew they were flimsy and fated for destruction, but the act of protest itself felt important. We needed defense mechanisms to keep us and our parties and our old ways of being together safe in the midst of a swelling tide.

Our efforts proved temporary, as we knew they would. Now the memory of them feels as primitive as those little brass mailboxes. Because today, of course, every party is a Facebook party, even if it has nothing whatsoever to do with Facebook.

⁓⁓⁓⁓

I've spent the past couple of years thinking about parties. All that thinking has come as a direct consequence of not experiencing any: I haven't attended a party for some time now and my interest in them has sharpened as a result. What were parties, I have found myself asking, wondering, remembering? What can they be in the future? To what extent is our collective social survival bound up with the ability, or will, to experience them?

Parties were one very notable casualty of the COVID-19 pandemic though, it must be said, they were a pretty trifling one. Compared to the more than one million American lives that were lost, the lack of parties felt like something that was not worth grieving over or complaining about. Life goes on, after all, with or without them, which is not something that can be said of real, human loss. If life goes on in the wake of such loss, it does so brokenly, with great effort and pain. What is a party in the face of such anguish.

But multiple years spent under the shadow of the coronavirus have felt, at least to me, like years lived entirely within that last couple of hours before a party you're throwing is scheduled to start. It's been years of pacing, of overthinking certain details, of nervous questioning: Who will show first? Is there enough booze? Are the snacks right? *Will anyone come?* What's worse, these feelings have intensified with time, sprouting sharper edges and a more lethal energy. Mild social anxiety has blossomed into full-fledged fear. A party, after all, is a gamble; it courts both opportunity and disaster. This is why we find parties thrilling, some of us. It's also why many of us dread them.

Parties may well constitute the apex of hanging out, but I think our collective contemporary feeling toward them is a bit mixed and complicated. It's true that absence makes the heart grow fonder, that it can bring about and inspire a kind of sentimental distortion. But it's also true that distance can make a thing, whatever it is, *stranger*. The farther away one stands from something, the more impossible it becomes to see that thing without the complement of its larger context. Suddenly, that context takes up the majority of the view, rendering the object in question small and insignificant. What we thought mattered most suddenly doesn't matter at all. Suddenly, the context itself is everything.

Raymond Williams, the Welsh critic and novelist known for his research into the social contextualization of language, among other topics, returned from fighting in World War II in 1945 to resume his studies at Cambridge. It was at that time that he found himself increasingly drawn to questions about the links between national consciousness and vocabulary. In the introduction to his monumental volume *Keywords*, which he published several decades later, in 1976, Williams describes how, in the years after the war, he became a cognizant of a sort of linguistic and cultural rift. "The fact is, they just don't speak the same language" was a phrase he heard repeated often.[1] But who was this "they"? The word, it turned out, referred to a range of divided populations: young people didn't "speak the same language" as their elders, working people didn't "speak the same language" as wealthy elites, soldiers who had been to war didn't "speak the same language" as those who had stayed behind.

Yet what Williams noticed was that this complaint, ostensibly one about language, was being used to shield a deeper conversation about mismatched social values. "When we come to say 'we just don't speak the same language,'" he writes, "we mean something more general: that we have different immediate values or different kinds of valuation, or that we are aware, often intangibly, of different formations and distributions of energy and interest."[2] Williams goes on to interrogate those "distributions of energy and interest" with regard to sixty common English language words, the meanings of which, as he saw it, were being renegotiated in light of changing social norms. Words like *community, family,* and *taste* were undergoing transformations that reflected the seismic cultural shifts occurring throughout the middle decades of the twentieth century. What's more, as Williams discovered, they had always done this, had always mutated during times of upheaval in order to make room for new social configurations.

Since I first read the book some fifteen years ago, Williams's *Keywords* has served as a kind of critical polestar for me. I return to it often, compelled by my appreciation for Williams's commitment to what feels like a series of experiments in willful overthinking. There is an obsessive quality to Williams's tracking of the permutations of the English language, but it is not for nothing: that obsessive brand of analysis stands in resistance to surface-level implications and one-sided thought. Williams works to draw out the multiple meanings of a word and, rather than sifting through and dividing them into piles of "right" and "wrong," he allows them to simply rest there in his open palm. It's a generous way of conducting research that does not view truth as a zero-sum game: no one is "wrong," in Williams's view. Rather, they are all participants in a shared process of meaning-making, a system by which language—and the range of human experience that language exists to name—gets endlessly remade and co-created.

Of parties, I now find it necessary to ask the same questions that Williams was asking of words like *community* back then, all those decades ago. That includes, as Williams puts it, "analy[zing] . . . some of the issues and problems that were there inside the vocabulary"[3]— working through all the conflicts that are to be found coiled up inside the words, that is, in order to access the truth. Often, that truth does not come in singular form but, rather, falls within a range of definitions that are imbued with the confidence and meanings of a particular historical moment. "Language depends, it can be said, on this kind of confidence," Williams argues, but "a necessary confidence and concern for clarity can quickly become brittle, if the questions involved are not faced."[4]

I think, for example, of all the parties I have ever attended that I didn't want to attend, or else where I attended only to devote much of my time to questions about my reasons for being there. *What am I doing here?* is a question I have nursed, in private, on numerous occasions and it's one I remain interested in because the answers are not hard and fast but, rather, to be found along a spectrum of psychological truth.

Once, at a colleague's going-away party, it was brought out into the open, this secret question of mine. Only I wasn't the one to ask it.

My colleague was leaving her job, which was also my job, for no job at all, having decided that she would rather relocate to rural Wisconsin with her fiancée and freelance than continue doing the kind of labor I myself had recently relocated across the country in order to commit myself to doing in her presence. Her choice didn't exactly offend me, but it prompted plenty of introspection. Her rejection of the thing that I had recently made sacrifices in order to obtain shone a spotlight on certain convictions that I had been taking for granted, or else been content to avoid. I was carrying these questions about my own convictions with me when I arrived at her going-away party, which took place at one of the swankier local bars in our town.

At the party, my colleague and I got into a discussion about how writers use social media for self-promotion. "Everybody uses social media for self-promotion," I remember saying. "But if you're only using it for self-promotion, you're doing it wrong."

I know that I said this at the time because it's something that I have often said, and often felt. In a world where every party is a

Facebook party—meaning that it comes with expectations about the public advertising and dispersal of essentially private acts—the idea of self-promotion starts to operate with the pernicious force of routine. But, over the years, I have worked to understand and see that routinization as a side effect of what life in a hyperconnected world looks like, and not as a worthy or desirable end in itself. The point is not to work toward self-promotion but to discover ways to live within a system that favors self-promotional tendencies while still carving out a space for what feels genuine and real. This is what I was trying to communicate to my colleague who, apparently, took personal offense at what I was saying.

Sensing judgment, she started into a flustered defense of her own social media habits. And then came the question: "Why are you *here?*"

I recall the pointed emphasis on the word *here*. As in, why are you in this room, right now, with me? She was demanding an explanation and I had only the most practical one to give in response.

"Because you invited me," I said.

It was at this moment that I realized two things: first, that my response was absolutely true, I was there solely for the sake of pleasing my colleague, who had invited me; second, that my colleague did not actually like me, which made my being there, and the prospect of my imagining that I could please her by being there, something of a conundrum.

This is what I meant when I said before that our collective contemporary feeling toward parties is a bit mixed and complicated. Parties are supposed to present opportunities for celebration and joy, yet they are often weighed down by other considerations, including those that arise from feelings of social responsibility. Sometimes a party is something we want, long for, and look forward to. But sometimes it can feel like something else: a duty, an obligation, a hostage situation, even.

Throughout the first several hundred years of the word's existence, *party* primarily referred to systems of separation. This continues to be the case with those words that are etymologically related to it through its root, the Latin word *partitum*, which means "that which is divided, shared, or allotted."[5] This original definition highlights the idea of communion through separation; a thing that is divided into parts is a thing that may then be shared among many. In the 1400s and 1500s, the word *party* was commonly used to designate parts of larger things, including kingdoms or countries. In Thomas Starkey's *A Dialogue Between Pole and Lupset* (more commonly known as *Starkey's England*, which dates from the 1520s or 1530s), one of the fictional speakers laments that nature has denied the people of England of fruits "wych grow in other partys,"[6] meaning other parts of the world. Also around this time, the word *party* was branching off in another direction and being used to refer to groups of people who had something in common, such as an opinion or political cause. Uses of the word dating since the 1400s define a party as "Those who are on one side in a contest, etc., considered collectively," according to the *Oxford English Dictionary*.[7] It is from this use of the word that we get *political parties*, which is what we call factions participating in a political contest. Thus we see that the history of *party* is marked by a tension between communion and partition, with the word sometimes favoring one or the other side in that definitional tug-of-war.

In fact, it wasn't until the eighteenth century—the period that saw the birth of modernity as we know it and also the beginnings of capitalism as we know it—that the word *party* started to be regularly associated with celebratory occasions. It had existed for centuries in close proximity to its etymological cousins, *part* and *partition*, sometimes getting conflated with them. But then, in the 1700s, it started to take on a range of more favorable connotations. The popular eighteenth-century author Eliza Haywood, also an accomplished translator of foreign-language literature, uses the word *party* in this new, celebratory context in her translation of *La Belle Assemblée*, by the French novelist Madeleine-Angélique de Gomez, better known simply as Madame de Gomez. The novella narrates, in fanciful and ultimately fictional terms, interpretations of historical events involving ancient European royalty. One of them, King Ethelred of Wessex, a real person who ruled the southern portions of modern-day England for a brief period between 865 and 871, is described sojourning from London "into the Country, on a Party of Pleasure with some of his Nobles."[8] Here, in Haywood's translation of Gomez's work, we see the word *party* perched upon something of a historical tipping point. On the one hand, it is still referring to a group of people who exist at a distance, or apart, from others—in this case, Ethelred and his company of nobles. On the other, though, the qualifying phrase "of Pleasure" tells us that the word is in the process of taking on new meanings relating to leisure. As with previous uses of the word *party*, it refers here to a group of people who have a cause in common, only now that cause is pleasure itself.

What's also clear, given this history of the word *party*, is a wider legacy of privilege. A "Party of Pleasure" is a project that requires time and resources. As such, it is a project that is only available to those who are privileged enough to possess plenty of both. In

Haywood's translation of Gomez's novella, King Ethelred embarks on his "Party of Pleasure" while his royal subjects, commoners lacking access to time and capital alike, line the street in throngs to "behold him pass." Ethelred acknowledges the devotion of his peasant subjects by "very often rais[ing] his head . . . to show himself with more Convenience to those in the Windows."[9] He makes a show, in other words, of both his leisure and his resources, performing for the sake of an audience of commoners that is unlikely to ever experience either.

In this way, the history of parties—and, indeed, the history of the word *party* itself—becomes tangled up with a history of privilege, which is to say, of economic class. When we think of the great partyers and party-goers of history, we tend to think of those who commanded opulence and wealth, like Marie Antoinette. These historic persons, true to the history of the word *party*, used their wealth to set themselves apart, to create space and erect fortifications between themselves and others. They gave themselves over to the art of pleasure by partition, which explains how the word *party* likewise became associated with exclusivity. A party is a device to unite and join, but it is also one that can be used to create or else reinforce conditions of separation. An invitation beckons to its target audience and, at the same time, announces to others that they are not welcome.

No wonder parties have the power to make us anxious. They are from their very roots, and even on the level of language, steeped in the stuff of anxiety.

"I sure do want this party to turn out all right. I sure do."

These are Mick Kelly's thoughts. She is the thirteen-year-old girl who, though not quite a protagonist, commands much of the reader's attention in Carson McCullers's 1940 novel *The Heart Is a Lonely Hunter*. Mick is on the cusp of throwing her first party. It's down to the last two hours before it's supposed to start, that famously agonizing period of time I mentioned earlier, and Mick is beset by doubts. She worries about the decorations: she walks out onto the porch of her family's home and then back inside again, in an effort to appraise them with fresh eyes. "There was plenty decoration. It was O.K.,"[10] she decides, though "O.K." is not going to be good enough for what she has planned.

To throw a party is a very grown-up thing and Mick Kelly is dead set on being an adult, despite her relatively young age. She dresses up in her older sisters' clothing for the party—the dress is too big, the shoes are too small—and restricts the guest list by age. No one under thirteen is allowed and that includes her younger siblings and neighbors, the people she is most accustomed to spending time with. She's looking to make new friends and, by extension, *re*make herself through this party of hers. It is to be a gathering composed not of friends but of vague acquaintances, people who say "I don't know you" when she calls on the phone to invite them, or else who have her repeat her name over and over again.[11] For Mick, this party is a foray into new territory: adulthood, maturity, and a dawning awareness of the conditions of separation that seem to only develop and deepen with age. The biggest one, for Mick, is class.

I said before that parties often amount to exercises in privilege. This one, Mick's party, is about the opposite—about not commanding privilege and not knowing it and then slowly, through a series of painful trials, coming to know it. It is through her party that Mick begins to understand and perceive her own poverty. It's a theme that surfaces repeatedly throughout McCullers's book, which was written at the tail end of the Great Depression. In order to grow up, Mick has to come to terms with everything she is not and with all that is, due to the circumstances of class, off limits to her. It's an excruciating journey but also one that would have resonated with many readers in 1940, as it continues to do today.

Mick's party is a "prom" party, meaning that it is structured around the activity of promenading, as opposed to dancing. Boys and girls fill out prom cards, which are like dance cards, and then pair up to take walks around the block. While Mick is out promenading with her neighbor, Harry Minowitz, one of the only boys who asks her, the poorer kids from the neighborhood invade and crash the party. Mick returns and surveys the damage they have wrought to her carefully managed, exclusive event:

> When she left the people were standing around in the fine clothes and it was a real party. Now—after just five minutes— the place looked more like a crazy house. While she was gone those kids had come out of the dark and right into the party itself . . . They bellowed and ran and mixed with the invited people—in their old loose-legged knickers and everyday clothes.[12]

The thing is, everybody at the party, and that includes both Mick's family members and the neighborhood kids who lay siege to it, *are having a good time.* The only one who isn't is Mick, and it's only because the party has run afoul of her plans for it.

Eventually, she gives herself over to the prospect of having a good time and induces everyone to go play in the ditch of a nearby construction site. But she stumbles jumping into it and ends up on her back in the mud, with the wind knocked out of her. No one, she realizes, has even noticed. Dejectedly, she makes her way back to the part where she kicks everyone out and sends them home. The party is not a success for Mick—not because it isn't fun, but because her anxiety about doing it right, about throwing the *right kind* of party, ruins it for her. She wanted to use it as an occasion to act like someone other than herself, but she catches herself acting like all that she really is: a poor kid.

I'm interested in what it means to party during difficult times. If parties may be viewed as high points of living—as apexes of hanging out—then it stands to reason that we might look to them when life proves particularly hard. But how does one do that? How is a person supposed to muster the energy and enthusiasm for a party when faced with the all the immediate concerns presented by hardship?

Mick Kelly's party in *The Heart Is a Lonely Hunter* takes place during the Great Depression. It's not a positive experience for Mick because she had hoped to use it to achieve something specific and she sees herself as having failed to do that. But that doesn't mean it isn't fun. After the neighborhood kids crash the event, Mick reflects, "The idea of the party was entirely over now. This was just regular playing-out. But it was the wildest night she had ever seen . . . [it] made all the other people forget about high school and being almost grown."[13] Mick notices that her party inspires a neglect for the responsibilities of age. This is important because, in Mick's small southern town, to be an adult is to be depressed—both in an emotional and spiritual sense (one of the main adult characters is so depressed and socially isolated, he later commits suicide) and also in a larger, cultural, and economic sense.

The Great Depression, as it was known, was dubbed "great" owing to its size and reach. It extended all across the United States and even into such communities as Mick's. But the effects of this chapter of history were chiefly felt by economic agents, meaning workers and wage earners—meaning adults. To kids like Mick, that experience was often reduced to mere background. Poverty and want were inarguable facts of life for children as well as adults, sure, but kids weren't likely to feel personally responsible for fixing them. Part of what McCullers's novel tries to do is draw a narrative map marking Mick's transition from a kid, meaning someone who is permitted to ignore the harsh realities of life during the Great Depression, to an adult, meaning someone who has no choice but to confront them. The party becomes a kind of pin on that map. It marks the last place that Mick is allowed to revel in the experience of childish enjoyment, the last place that she knows what it means to have fun.

In 1939, the same year that McCullers was writing *The Heart Is a Lonely Hunter*, the English writer Henry Green published his novel *Party Going*. It's about a fictional group of people in their twenties associated with the "Bright Young Things" set, which was a name given to real-life, elite revelers whose exploits filled the British tabloid magazines of the 1920s and '30s. In Green's novel, the group is on their way to a party, but they become stranded at a London railway station on account of fog. They wait out the weather at the station hotel, where they gather "in desperate good humor"[14] and try (but not too hard) to have a good time. That involves fending off a series of existential crises that result from not having any parties to be at. The irony of the situation, of course, is that Green's characters are all there together. They constitute a group, a faction, a *party*, in a technical and pure sense. But they are not where parties are supposed to take place for people like them, and this makes them miserable. They while away the hours in stylish despair, blocked from accessing aesthetically rich scenes that exist to make life more meaningful or, perhaps, to shield them from the meaninglessness of the lives they have built for themselves.

Between McCullers and Green, then, we have two snapshots of what it was like to party in the year 1939, in the midst of the Great Depression, or the "Great Slump" as it was known in England. Though ostensibly quite different, and with a whole ocean separating their respective authors, these two novels engage in a simultaneous and historically specific contemplation of hanging out, something akin to what Raymond Williams calls a "structure of feeling." Williams uses this term to identify artistic works that express a similar historical worldview, or else encapsulate and respond to a shared set of "palpable pressures,"[15] as he calls them. A structure of feeling unites two artistic works though the artists or authors in question may have nothing in common and no working knowledge of each other.

This is the case with McCullers and Green, two authors that were both interested in and, perhaps, worried about the social isolation wrought by the Great Depression. McCullers's snapshot of the year 1939 is a bleak one: in it, we see dirty children, residents of a Southern American backwater, living it up on what feels like the last night of their childhood. Green's snapshot, meanwhile, appears more glitzy and composed, at least at first glance. His characters, who are essentially overgrown children, engage in witty debates about superficial concerns. They argue, for instance, over the social acceptability of helping oneself to a host's liquor store and mixing up a cocktail from it while that host is absent. (It is okay to do this, they decide, so long as it doesn't involve opening a bottle of champagne.)[16] But all that repartee serves to disguise feelings of social awkwardness and ineptitude. By the time the fog lifts and the trains start running again, the time spent together in close quarters has caused many of their relationships to sour, making the prospect of the party they were bound for feel less worthwhile. Their party-going, Green suggests, has been revealed for what it is: a means of evasion. What they were really seeking, all along, was not a good time, or even a respite from the world of the Great Depression, but activity for activity's sake, to keep them busy and perpetually distracted. Their ceaseless quest for distraction ends up exposing them to the vacuous truth of normal life.

When I, as an American schoolchild, learned about the Great Depression, I didn't hear about the parties. I think I had assumed for a period of maybe ten or so years, there were no parties—that a party moratorium, maybe, came into effect along with rationing and other austerity measures. Yet those parties existed and they abound in literature and artistic works dating from the period. For instance, in William McPherson's sumptuous novel *Testing the Current*, which was published in 1984 but looks back upon the period of his childhood in the late 1930s, there is a long crescendo toward a party that comes at the very end of the book. When it does, it's a grand affair, a wedding anniversary dance staged in a country club

setting. The whole point is to guide the reader through the historical era of the Depression so that they can arrive at the party ready
to relish the contrast. Likewise, in Tess Slesinger's *The Unpossessed*
(1934), one of my favorite novels of the 1930s, there are plenty of
parties, all of them seemingly overflowing with gin cocktails, even
as the characters plot out paths toward political insurgency, inspired
by dire economic circumstances.

Seen in this way, through the lens of a period like the Great
Depression, a party starts to look not simply like a means of distraction from the various hazards of reality but also like a survival
mechanism. A party instills a pause that, sometimes, works to delay
the inevitable and allows its participants to rest and plan. A party
gathers people together and grants them temporary shelter within
the space of that pause. A party cannot solve the problems of the
world, of course, but it can be the spark that sets the fires of courage burning for those who must face those problems.

Whatever the occasion that prompts it, a party is about hope. We
throw parties—"offer" them, in the words of Virginia Woolf's Mrs.
Dalloway, one of literature's pre-eminent partyers[17]—in order to
fashion containers for the preservation of hope. Even the verb we
use to encapsulate that action, throw, is suggestive of tossing a life
preserver into open water. A party is a place to park our dreams.
We stuff our parties full of the things that we desire most from the
world: sex, desirability, social companionship, indulgence, freedom
from consequences. Then we go back to the real work, which is the
work of living, and we wait for the next one to come around.

Back when I was in college, I think our parties were all about hope. This was as much true when they had nothing to do with Facebook as when they did. Those parties were where we practiced and performed our skills as fledgling adults. They included elaborate theme and costumes parties because this was in rural Ohio, a place that forces a person to make her own fun, and also because dressing up is sacred to the work of performance itself.

I recall, for instance, one of the last parties I ever attended on campus, which took place during the last week of my senior year. Some friends of mine had concocted a plan for a final costume party. The theme of it was pointedly aspirational: dress as the person you will be in ten years.

It poured down rain that night, the sort of rain that used to bend the lilacs down to the ground and scatter their blossoms across the sidewalks of campus. I was dressed in all tweed, having cobbled together a Goodwill outfit (there was nothing unusual about that; all my clothes came from Ohio Goodwill stores back then, with the result being that I was usually dressed like a seventies grandmother crossed with maybe a rodeo veteran). I showed up soaking wet, wearing what felt like ten pounds of wet wool. A friend of mine, Adrianne, was dressed like a kindergarten teacher, in a smock that had finger paint smeared all over the front of it. Last I heard, she's teaching preschool in Portland.

These costumes of ours, they were engineered for evasion yet they spoke fluently in terms of exposure. We were using them to communicate and advertise our hopes for the future—well, some of us, anyway (an old friend, Kacie, who helped organize the party, has since informed me that many of the costumes weren't devised with earnestness in mind, prompting me to wonder, sheepishly: *Was*

I always this earnest?). I hoped that in ten more years, I would have realized my dream of being a college professor. I had dressed up as something I was not in order to reveal something that I wanted very badly, something I was scared of trying for, because it is a very terrifying thing to have to try.

In *The Heart Is a Lonely Hunter*, Mick Kelly stops trying after her party leaves her feeling dejected. She casts off the clothing she borrowed from her sisters, removes her makeup, and resumes her old uniform, which includes a pair of shorts. As she does this, she reflects that she is doing so for the last time. "She was too big to wear shorts any more after this. No more after this night. Not any more."[18] Then, after the party scene, McCullers's novel takes a turn, swerving hard toward the cold truths of maturity for characters like Mick. By the end of the book, Mick has dropped out of school and started a job at Woolworth's, earning a wage that amounts to a pittance but feels like a fortune to a girl of fourteen. In the final scene, she shows up at the local café after a shift and orders, tragically, two items from the menu. One of them, a chocolate sundae, is made for a child and the other, a beer, is made for an adult. It's a combination that shows Mick still caught between those two worlds, and it always puts a twist in my heart.

Back in Ohio in 2005, at my friends' aspirational costume party, I felt exposed because I knew that I was announcing my intentions in a very public way. I had dressed in three pieces of tweed, on a hot and stormy May night, not because I had ever seen a college professor of mine actually dress that way but because I knew the outfit spoke in the way I wanted it to and said the things I was still afraid of saying out loud, to myself or anyone else. I worried that I wouldn't be good enough to get up close and touch the things that

I wanted. I was still many years and multiple degrees away, after all. But my fears proved smaller than the seductions of hope. I wanted to gather together with my friends, to squeeze into a dorm room for one last time in order to bask in those collectively generated currents of optimism. I was using a performative gesture in order to feel the weight of the future in my hand, to test whether it might be possible after all.

In 2014, I got a job as a college professor and moved to North Dakota. There, I lived in a town where it seemed that every party was an invitation to imagine life somewhere else. Those parties were like spells or incantations. They conjured up romanticized and aesthetically unimpeachable visions of distant locales and exotic elsewheres. Most of them were places where my colleagues, the people who threw these parties, had lived before they came to this, the place where we all now lived together. As a result, these parties, though they were certainly about hope, were about the particular kind of hope that is gleaned from memory.

For example, there was the annual Mardi Gras party. My friends Paul and Michelle hosted this party each year in acknowledgment of their shared geographic heritage (as young professionals, they had spent a few years living in New Orleans). In time, I came to see their Mardi Gras party as a kind of anchor point within a larger, annual calendar of festive elsewheres. It set into motion a long season of dreaming about places that were not North Dakota and what's more, it did so during the month of February.

For those living within striking distance of the 49th parallel, let alone *above* it, that month comes as an annual low point. February is the bottom of the whole, big barrel that is winter—the dregs, the droppings, the sludgy sediment of the year's calendrical brutality. In North Dakota, February would come down like a sledgehammer, burying the town in a succession of waist-deep snows. The pace of life would then slacken, with the early evenings and dark nights holding steady. It became hard to move, hard to see each other, hard to remember what life beyond February felt like. Neighbors might die or be born during February and you might not find out until spring, so complete was the month's cloistering effect on everyone.

But then came Mardi Gras, every year, just when we needed it— needed an elsewhere—most. The living room at Paul and Michelle's house would be ankle-deep with beads, the cheap plastic kind that get tossed into the crowd during Mardi Gras parades and then linger into the summer and fall tangled up in trees lining the streets of the French Quarter. Paul and Michelle had garbage bags full of those beads stored away in their attic. Neighborhood kids would be on all fours, swimming through the sea of beads while, in the kitchen, adults would gather to talk and sip hurricanes. In the dining room, pushed up against one wall, the big table would be crowded with dishes: king cake and jambalaya and red beans and rice and whatever else guests had brought to contribute. Propped somewhere near it would be the night's most honored guest, a man dressed in clerical garb and known only as The Cardinal, who was actually the subject of an oversized, gilt-framed oil portrait that Paul and Michelle had once haphazardly acquired and then started bringing along with them to the bars on their annual Mardi Gras rounds. Everyone at the party had to pose for a photo with The Cardinal.

These were not all-night ragers. None of us had the stamina for anything like that. But the Mardi Gras party generally lasted until midnight or one in the morning, at which point a kind of distillation would occur. Only a few people would remain, and my partner Dave and I were always among them. This smaller group would relocate away from the dining room with its picked-over carcass of a king cake and its leaning towers of dishes. We would settle into some leather couches positioned near the kitchen. We would switch from hurricanes to straight bourbon as Paul and Michelle told stories about their years in New Orleans, about the various parades, the concerts they saw, the places they loved, and The Cardinal's fabled origins. These stories would spin out and hook up with others, like the one about the time when Paul got caught by a blizzard on I-89 and spent the better part of a day trapped in his car in the company of a bunch of his own graduate students. These were stories of other times and other parties, essentially, but they served to kindle a new and deeper kind of intimacy. They helped to make us see that this party, our party, was the offspring of all those past parties and thus connected in a long chain of faded social linkages.

When the talk would get slow and the yawns would get more frequent, we would all go our separate ways again, plunging back out into the snow as Paul and Michelle waved from their porch. Dave and I would usually walk because our town was not that big and so even in February, walking from place to place was always an option, if you were brave enough. For the first few blocks, we might have company in the form of other friends who had stayed late at the party. But then they would peel off onto their own streets and it would be just the two of us, struggling toward home in the midst of whatever February had thought to serve up that night—howling winds, sheet ice, a few fresh inches of new snow, or maybe some combination of all of these. I remember a friend of ours, once, down on his back on the icy sidewalk, covered in the quinoa salad he and his wife had brought to the party, howling with laughter. It took all three of us to get him upright and on his feet again.

We lived there for six years, Dave and I, and we never missed the Mardi Gras party. It was our favorite annual elsewhere. It, and the other parties like it, helped to fortify and guide us through those long, cold seasons of stagnancy. Those periodic gatherings were like knots on a rope that we would feel for in the dark and then grab onto. We counted on them to pull us back toward the light.

After the Mardi Gras party came the rest. Snow would often last well into May in North Dakota and, by mid-April, I could expect to find myself huddled around a steaming kettle positioned on the bank of a frozen lake. That was another colleague's party, an annual crawfish boil. Then there was the infamous, Spanish-themed paella party that came around at the start of spring each year, hosted by a colleague who happened to own a 60-inch paella pan. I never got invited to that party, because it was a Facebook party, but I always heard plenty about it from those who did.

There's a poem by Audre Lorde that is about dying slowly while, on the other side of the wall, a party takes place. Somehow, it is not a sad poem, or at least it is not primarily sadness that rings out and surfaces as its dominant note. The poem is called "The Electric Slide Boogie" and it describes an annual, festive occasion: New Year's. It's a less festive one for the poem's speaker, though, whose circumstances seem to invite comparison to Lorde's own. In 1992, when she wrote the poem, she was dying of cancer.

What I love about this poem is its attitude of joyful resistance. Though she cannot join them, the poem's speaker refuses
to begrudge others their parties and celebrations. Instead, she pays
tribute to the ecstasy of those celebrations in a voice that is both
filled with longing and yet never quite fully envious. She will not
allow what little time or energy she has left to burn up or be consumed by a searing jealousy.

In the poem, it is just after one o'clock in the morning where
the speaker is but "it is midnight in Idaho" and noise is erupting
from a television broadcast in deference to this fact. Alongside the
noise emanating from the TV is a cacophony of real sound, present
sound, which fills the room next door to the speaker. Lorde mentions that her partner, Gloria, is among the throng gathered there.
Lorde's speaker cannot be part of that cacophony, but she can
relax into the hearing of sounds made by people she loves. They
are ordinary sounds of ordinary people who are celebrating the
New Year—celebrating the onset of a new, annual instance of the
future—in very ordinary ways, with clinking glasses, forks scraping against plates, conversation and laughter. There is also dancing.
People doing the electric slide boogie go "step-stepping / around
the corner of the parlor."[19] But who? Is it the people nearby, in the
living room? Is it the people on TV, in Idaho? Does it matter?

Lorde refuses to make a distinction between the two groups—
between real and projected experience, between witnessing and
participating. Instead, she has her speaker reflect on the experience
of bodily exhaustion and the feeling of being "weary beyond /
time." That exhaustion stands in contrast to the exuberance that is happening, either literally or figuratively, on the other side of the wall from

her. The speaker's body keeps telling her to sleep. But she resists its instructions all the way up to the end, where she offers a parting observation. "How hard it is to sleep / in the middle of life."[20]

That's where Lorde leaves her speaker in this poem, still resisting, still "in the middle" of things, including all the sonic mess of life. She is caught on the threshold between the party that summons her with its noise and the demands of her own ailing body. It's also where Lorde leaves her reader since, in *The Collected Poems of Audre Lorde* (1997), "The Electric Slide Boogie" comes last, being one of the last ones she wrote (though, significantly, not *the* last, a fact that calls attention to the decision to place it at the end of the volume). Every time I flip to the last page and arrive at it, I am overcome with awe for this woman whose last word to the living world is, effectively, a command to keep going, keep partying, keep celebrating, and difficult times be damned.

This, I think, is what a party does, or at least what it has the potential to do. It gathers people together and offers a chance "to combine, to create,"[21] to quote from Virginia Woolf once more. What gets combined are the raw elements of human social existence. What gets created is momentum, a rhythmic energy pushing us toward whatever comes next.

2 HANGING OUT WITH STRANGERS

She is surrounded by people and yet, it's obvious: she is alone.

It's her darting gaze that gives her away and alerts us to the fact of her loneliness. It's itinerant; it does not rest or stick anywhere. It seeks and then gives up, turning inward as she closes her eyes and moves more deeply into the music and the motions of her own body. She dances by herself—not brazenly, not obliviously, but carefully, maintaining a safe little circle of space around her. She makes small, nervous adjustments that speak to her continued awareness of her body in that space, of its vulnerability. She fusses with her hair, arranging it into a ponytail while her feet keep the rhythm. She smiles to herself, shyly, in a way that signals her desire to share that smile with others.

A crescendo builds, the song changes. She moves to exit the dance floor, her motions retaining all that energy and joy but, at the same time, still edged in faint shades of caution. The camera follows her out of the room and into the one adjoining it. There, she plants her elbows on the bar and leans forward in an effort to capture the bartender's eye. It takes a few seconds but then he approaches. She speaks in English but uses the German word, *schnapps*. The bartender pours the shot and she ventures a few more words of German, clearly approaching the limits of her vocabulary in that language: *Danke schön*.

Switching back to English, she asks if he would like to join her, using her hands to say what her words cannot. Shots are party drinks, not meant to be consumed alone. She's offering to buy the bartender a beverage in exchange for a few seconds' worth of his company. She awaits his answer with eyes that are large and unsure. When it comes, we can see it in her face, that flicker of disappointment. Her hair falls forward as she bends to her drink. She shoots it back under the curtain of her hair and then coughs slightly, glancing around to see if anyone's noticed.

This is how we meet Victoria. She is the protagonist in a film of the same name, a 2015 German-language thriller directed by Sebastian Schipper and starring Spanish actress Laia Costa.[1] *Victoria* tracks its young namesake's movements across the city of Berlin over the course of a single, tumultuous, and life-changing night. Victoria is a stranger there, having relocated from her native Spain, and she is desperate to discover social inclusion. That desperation is written all over her interactions with the bartender, which occur about five minutes into the film. Conventional wisdom might hold that the last person who ever needs, or stands to benefit from, an offer of a free drink is the person whose job it is to sell drinks in the first place. Thus we see Victoria's gaffe with the bartender as driven by a sad sort of urgency. When he rebuffs her offer, her big, brown eyes radiate a look of isolation.

She rallies, though. Her ponytail whips back and forth as she scans her surroundings, rises, and heads for the restroom. On her way there, she exchanges brief words with a stranger, a young man who is loitering near the door with a group of friends. They are trying to gain admission to the club she's in. This is the beginning of everything that is going to happen to her.

Victoria is a film about hanging out with strangers—about seeking intimacy and social inclusion, finding it, and then following it all the way down to a dark and calamitous end. The film is notable for making use of a single, continuous shot, or filmic "take," which lasts for more than two hours. This means that the camera and the camera operator, much like the actors, never gets to rest. There are no pauses or interruptions as it follows the winsome Victoria and her companions throughout the streets of a pre-dawn Berlin. When they run, the camera runs with them, sometimes struggling to keep pace; when they pile into a stolen van, the camera is there, too, sandwiched between them in the back seat. The camera's constant insertion within the action of the film is the audience's insertion and also Victoria's. The viewer has no choice but to go along for the ride and find out where it leads.

In this way, the film captures the thrill that, often, gilds the surface of another feeling: peril. Both are endemic to the experience of hanging out with strangers. There is an irresistible sense of allure and fascination, a feeling of anything-can-happen-here, because if you don't know a person you can't know exactly what to expect from them. Victoria feels it: that's why she follows the young man and his friends up the stairs of the club and out into the street and why she ignores the warning signs that, slowly, one by one, start to amass around her.

The first one comes with a joke about stealing a car. The moment passes, though: the car's owner shows up, the tension is briefly dissolved, and the group moves on. But then, in a *Späti*, another opportunity presents itself. *Späti* are convenience stores that sell beer at all hours and thus serve as a cornerstone of public drinking culture in Berlin. Victoria follows the character Sonne inside one, where they find the store's proprietor asleep at the register. Sonne indicates his intentions to steal the beer rather than paying for it and Victoria, after a second's hesitation, goes along with the plan, even pocketing some snacks on her way out. This is an important moment in the film: it records a minor transgression on Victoria's part but also hints at how far she might be willing to go in order to be accepted by a bunch of people she has just met.

Anyone who has ever ventured out alone—ever braved new surroundings or sought company in a room full of total strangers—knows how it feels to be Victoria. They know what it is to weigh a minor ethical infraction against the prospect of a few hours' worth of inclusion. It's a scenario that harkens back to the essential things of life, to childhood and the school playground's cauldron of cruelty and peer pressure. But, as the film shows, it's something that doesn't necessarily disappear with age. It's an urge that can lay dormant for years when presented with only familiar faces and scenes. But come a strange city, a new context, a lonely night, a random bar, a vacuous hotel room, a second language, a halting conversation, a casual introduction—come any combination of these things, and that old playground urge can come roaring back to life again.

There is no amount of maturity that can be stockpiled in defense. There is no way of avoiding it except by staying home and avoiding the world.

Once, I could have been Victoria.

More than once, maybe. But I'm thinking of a particular instance, one that took place years ago in Scotland. As an undergraduate, I was lucky enough to study abroad during my junior year. An exchange program placed me at the University of Aberdeen, where I was able to keep doing what I had been doing back in the United States at my small Ohio college and, significantly, where I was also able to play my bagpipes. This was part of the plan, see; my scholarship, which paid me to go to school in exchange for my work as a bagpiper, also covered the costs of my time in Scotland, or some of them anyway. In Aberdeen, I joined a local pipe band, ventured out nightly to participate in jam sessions hosted by local pubs, and made weekly trips down to Glasgow for lessons at the renowned Piping Centre. And I made friends; I stepped into friendships as readily as I did puddles littering the rainy streets, without first assessing their depths. Then I went back to Ohio, because I had to.

A few years later, one of those friends invited me to attend her wedding, which was to take place in Scotland in August. The night before I was scheduled to leave, though, I suffered an injury (a tent stake through the foot, a long story that is barely related to this one but too bizarre not to mention in passing) that made air travel impossible. So I saved my flight credit and resolved to travel the following winter, over New Year's, to visit my friend and her new husband.

But there were complications. My friend and her husband were going to be on vacation in Greece over New Year's but returning a few days later. My travel voucher, meanwhile, was only good through December 31. So my friend offered to let me stay in her apartment in Aberdeen until they returned, at which point we could all spend a few days together. This is how I ended up alone in Aberdeen, a city that I thought I knew until I ended up alone in it.

I was young. I don't think I felt it then, but I know it now. Twenty-three is young. And I was traveling alone. I had done so before, which made the whole plan feel less risky and audacious from the outset. The differences soon revealed themselves, though: it wasn't about traveling alone but about what I would or would not find when I got there. I was traveling alone to a place where I would likewise *be* alone. There was no one waiting for me on the other side, no one preparing for my arrival, no one to offer words of advice or greeting. This did not bother me until it did.

My original flight, the one I had booked back in the summer, had been for Glasgow, not Aberdeen. So that's where I arrived on a cold, clear morning in late December, carrying only a backpack. It contained a single change of clothes, a digital camera, a few books, and a wedding gift for my friend. From Glasgow, I boarded a train to Aberdeen, just as I had done every single Tuesday for months and months on end when I lived there and commuted once a week to Glasgow for my lessons.

I arrived in Aberdeen after an absence of three years feeling like an utter stranger, to both the place and to myself. Though I had worked to keep some of my former friendships alive through long-distance methods, a lot of my friends had scattered during the interim—either temporarily on account of the holidays, or more permanently on account of life changes. This was before social media; this was before the most minor of intimacies came burdened with expectations of forced permanence. I didn't even have a cell phone to help me navigate my surroundings.

But I didn't really need one. I discovered that I still held the names of streets and landmarks in my head and could easily get around. "There is a peculiar voluptuousness in the naming of streets," notes the philosopher Walter Benjamin.[2] Writing in the early 1900s, he's talking about the historical process by which a city gets mapped, charted, and tamed, largely through the assigning of names. To name is to know, to assert mastery, which is one of the first principles of structuralist philosophy. Though he died before finishing it, Benjamin's *The Arcades Project* is his magnum opus—a work of more than a thousand pages devoted to musings and hoarded quotations about modernity, urbanity, and the disordered entanglements that result from the combination of the two. Benjamin compares the sprawling streets of Paris, his so-called "capital of the nineteenth century," to the entrails of a beast, to the lap of a whore, to the labyrinths of antiquity—things designed to ensnare and trap and enchant the wanderer, preventing forward movement.[3] Names, he reasons, become part of the machinery of subjugation, working to make the streets less perilous and wild. Identifying the names of streets in Aberdeen, repeating them to myself, gave me confidence. Moving through a landscape I could read helped me to bear the knowledge that not a single person in it recognized me.

On my first night in Aberdeen, I ventured out alone to a bar that I had remembered frequenting in the company of other students, years before. In the cold light of both my solitude and a slightly enhanced sense of maturity, I discovered it to be a pit of dejection—a grim little meat market that, because the university was on break, was also basically empty. The ensuing days were then devoted to long and relatively aimless perambulations. I roamed wintry beaches, picked my way through the cobblestoned lanes of campus, visited churches and cemeteries and parks. I was playing at Benjamin's notion of the *flâneur*, the urban wanderer who moves slowly enough to take in the whole monstrous human spectacle. If you go to graduate school for a degree in the humanities, the concept of the *flâneur* is one that you are not permitted to not imbibe. It reaches its apex in a tale—probably apocryphal but frankly delectable—of nineteenth-century men of leisure who would stroll through the Parisian arcades, which were like precursors to indoor malls, with turtles on leashes. The idea was that they could set their pace to the turtle and thus have a ready excuse for walking slowly, for loafing.

In Aberdeen, I had a camera, which is its own passport to leisurely pacing. I took pictures of beautiful, meaningless things: roses blooming in the middle of winter in front of St. Machar's, bridges spanning the half-frozen River Don, granite buildings glittering coldly in the sun, gulls astride tombstones in an urban graveyard. I was low on money and so trying to avoid spending what little I had on things like entertainment or food. That left plenty of room for the twin pastimes of walking and starving.

It's one thing, I think, to be alone when you are on your own turf, with access to friends or phone numbers or places and people that make sense. That kind of alone has it charms; it can be invigorating, especially if one's life has been arranged so as to usually deliver the opposite result. At twenty-three, solitude still felt like an achievement to me, like something that had to be fought for. I had weathered years of roommates and, just prior to leaving for Scotland, I'd been back at my family's house for the holidays, where the volume is permanently stuck at eleven. In Scotland, though, I was invisible in my solitude, faced with the realization that I had once come and gone from this city without leaving any kind of mark on it, socially speaking. Nobody who knew me knew I was there, save for someone who wasn't there herself; meanwhile, nobody who was there knew me. As I wandered the streets alone—first in exultation, then with increasing anxiety—I had plenty of time to question my reasons for coming.

I wanted to see my friend, to see if she was still my friend. I wanted to use the plane ticket I hadn't been able to use for her wedding. I wanted to pay back that lost opportunity to hang out on an important day of her life. I wanted to avoid the waste of all that money, because I had so little of it. I wanted to take advantage of something that was right there in front of me, to say yes to it. I wanted to be the kind of person who said yes. I wanted to make myself into the kind of person for whom yes always felt like an easy thing to do, a logical conclusion.

Being alone in my friend's apartment, though, didn't feel like yes. Rather, it felt like extricating myself from all social opportunities, rather than placing myself in the path of new, more exciting ones. My friend was married; she had a real job now; her life was heading somewhere else, away from the point where we had stood together as students and as friends back when we'd drank Malibu rum in that terrible underground student bar. Away from me, because I didn't live here anymore and had only barely done so before. In her silent, white, savagely IKEA-ed apartment, I found few recognizable traces of the person I remembered but, then again, I didn't have much to go on. I'd only seen the inside of her old student flat a handful of times. It had looked exactly like every other student flat I'd ever been in, including my own.

The novelist Rick Moody says in his wonderful *Hotels of North America* that blank spaces like hotel rooms—or, in my case, a friend's apartment in a foreign city—help us to "see the horizon, even if there is no land to be witnessed there."[4] They promote introspection and mental adjustment, which is maybe what is so terrifying about them. A person is never so much themselves as when they are alone in a hotel room. The same thing, it turned out, could be said for being alone in someone else's vacant apartment. I tried to remind myself that I was alone there only because I was waiting for the time to come when I wouldn't have to be. But under the doubled weight of all that expectation and memory, the days lasted for weeks and the nights for years.

Because I couldn't hang out with my friend, I tried my best to instead hang out with the city itself—to reclaim my relationship with the place in light of its inevitable and already quite pronounced unravelling. Then came New Year's Eve. I'd been on my own for four days by then. It wasn't that long but it felt interminable, those four days that had passed without a conversation that went beyond the purchase of a beverage. I couldn't stay home in my friend's empty apartment on New Year's Eve, I had to find people, strangers who would let me hang out.

She is surrounded by people and yet, it's obvious: she is alone.

You can tell by the way she smokes her cigarette, which is the way that a person smokes a cigarette when they are more inter- ested in killing time than ingesting nicotine. Her face is open and affable though her stance is anxious. She occupies a corner of the street, sticking close to the shadows of a nearby building and its overhanging roof, like she's trying to stay out of the rain except it's not raining. Her gaze, meanwhile, remains quietly evaluative. It skims the faces of the people who pass by, but rapidly, mindful of the line between interaction and confrontation. She's washed her hair and applied enough eyeliner to make it look like she has plans, intentions. But she doesn't. Not yet. She's smoking a cigarette on the corner at the top of Belmont Street, home to the busiest stretch of bars in Aberdeen, in the hopes of finding some.

It's early still but already very dark. Winter in Aberdeen is a tunnel of darkness, pierced by only the most occasional mercies—blinding blue days when the city's granite facades dazzle, or sometimes the northern lights. She remembers being in the kitchen of her old flat on Don Street once, a place she shared with three girls named Nicola and two guys not named Nicola. There was a radio that sat atop the refrigerator. The local station DJ was talking to them: *If you're in Aberdeen right now, get outside . . .* In the WC, there was a hatch that led up onto the roof. If you stood on the toilet, you could hoist yourself up. She remembers that one of the guys had to help boost the bunch of them, her and two of the Nicolas. And then there they were, the lights, smeared blue and green across the far edge of the sky, just visible above a black fringe of trees.

On the opposite corner now, a group of young men has appeared, three of them. Like her, they are waiting, but their eyes assess the passing crowd in search of something more specific. Also like her, they are smoking. She decides to try something—the oldest and most reliable trick in the smoker's handbook, but one that still feels novel to her. She puts out her half-smoked cigarette, mashing it with a bootheel, then marches across to the opposite corner. She smiles, shakes her pack of cigarettes, and asks for a light, though she of course has one in her pocket.

It works. One of them produces a lighter and holds the flame out to her. She bends toward it, tucking her hair protectively behind one ear. Though she has smoked for years now, she has never been at peace with her identity as a smoker and so remains prone to feeling like an impostor. As with most things, she is quick to convince herself that she is doing it wrong. She worries that this is obvious to others. Five years have elapsed since she started smoking and yet she still surprises herself with each new enactment of the charade.

The cigarette in her hand lights easily and a halting conversation ensues. The guys are waiting for a fourth friend who is going to join them tonight on a pub crawl. The fourth friend is called Mark and his is the only name she will remember later on. She waits with them and they don't appear to mind, appear glad to have her around, in fact. This is clear from the way they turn and face her when she speaks, offering up their attention as generously as they did the lighter. Maybe too generously. They give her their whole gazes instead of keeping part of them free, looking out for something better to come along down Belmont Street.

They are oil and gas workers, she learns. They work on the offshore rigs, the ones that light up the North Sea at night, looking like little cities marooned out there in the blue. They work for weeks straight at sea on the rigs, in exchange for which they get one uninterrupted week of dry land, sometimes more. This is their first night back and it's Hogmanay. Their plan is to hit every bar on Belmont Street and then some, to make up for the fact that they don't get to drink on the rigs. They invite her to join and she surprises herself by agreeing.

Mark shows up. He has short brown hair and endearingly crooked teeth that are exposed by a ready smile. Something about him feels a little broken, dented. He apologizes for being late: he had to stop by his parents' house first, which is where he lives when he doesn't live out on the rig. "Stays" is the word they use, not "lives," and it strikes her as the more appropriate of the two. "Live" feels freighted with a permanence she has never known; "stay," on the other hand, feels reasonably time-based and subject to change, which is the truth of life and living anyway.

As they walk in a pack to the first of many pubs, Mark asks lots of questions—about the city she's from, which he's heard of because of ketchup and football, and about what she's doing in Aberdeen. Some of the questions, like the last one, prove hard to answer. It's been four days and she has started to forget.

At the second pub, two women join them and she feels relieved. The whole group orders and pays in rounds, as is the custom, and pools the change in a kitty which Mark keeps in his coat pocket.

By the third, they're developing in-jokes and communal phraseology.

At the fourth, one of the guys, who goes by a nickname that's a reference to some sort of dessert (Cake? Cookie? Fudge?), slips an arm about her waist and pulls her close. His embrace feels slick as oil.

At the fifth pub, one of the women warns her—privately, in the ladies' room—about the dessert-named fellow, who apparently has a reputation. She didn't need to be warned.

Somewhere between the sixth and seventh pub, she stops at an ATM and withdraws every last dollar in her checking account without realizing that that is what she is doing.

The eighth pub is a local dive that is affectionately referred to as The Swamp, though that's not its name. It's located in a cellar and accessible via a flight of slippery stone stairs. The humidity inside causes her hair to curl, revealing the mystery behind its unofficial moniker.

By the ninth pub, they've exhausted all their options on Belmont Street and moved further afield.

Midnight strikes in the tenth pub and Mark kisses her.

By the eleventh pub, the other women have dropped out and it's just the five of them again.

At the twelfth pub, she remembers her camera and starts taking pictures, which is the only way she is later able to remember the twelfth pub.

At the thirteenth pub, or maybe it's the fourteenth, they are refused service and they tumble out in a knot onto Union Street and try to hail a cab.

There are no cabs, not on Hoggers. So they start walking.

There is a house party happening in some neighborhood that is far but not too far, apparently. One of the guys has bottles of Stella stored in his coat and he passes them around and no one asks how they got there. She thinks she knows the direction they are heading, toward Garthdee, but she's not sure. Years before, she'd briefly dated a fiddler who lived there; he played the Monday night sessions at a pub called the Blue Lamp, which is where they met, and she can recall the exact price of a cab ride back to Don Street from his flat. Once, she'd hailed a cab barefoot because she was late for class and hadn't been able to find her shoes. The fiddler, he ended up breaking her heart when he got back together with an old girlfriend, but that hadn't stopped her from sending him a Christmas card every year. She has, in fact, recently done so, again.

Halfway to Garthdee, or wherever it is they're heading, a cab stops. There's not enough room for all of them, though, so she stays back with Mark and together, they keep walking. They stop at a SPAR for more Stella, which Mark carries in a plastic bag. It's a long way to the house and it's cold, but they're walking slowly with beers and cigarettes in hand. At some point, Mark starts to talk about his ex; at some point, she starts to realize that "ex" means *ex-wife*, that he's recently divorced, though he's only two years older than her. In fact not quite all the way divorced yet. The alcohol shelters her from having to form solid opinions about this.

It takes them an hour or more to reach the house and the party is so loud there that no one can hear them knocking. They keep trying, then give up and go around to the back to see if there's another door. There isn't, though they can see through the kitchen window: a squirming, violent barrage of bodies. They sit in the backyard and drink the Stella until someone eventually notices them and lets them in.

Inside is where the tone of the evening changes, starts to intensify and darken. The other guys are there but they seem different from how they were before, less good-humored and more edgy. She thinks it might be the drugs. She watches somebody do a line of cocaine off a framed photo of what turns out to be someone else's grandmother. She wonders what happened to the two other women, if they're here somewhere and she just can't see them. She loses track of Mark and spends fifteen minutes barricaded in the bathroom because it's the only place where the light is strong enough to cut through the seeping darkness. She's growing nervous, thinking about how she doesn't know where she is, how it might not even be Garthdee, she was so busy talking to Mark that she forgot to notice. She thinks about how easy it would be for her to vanish in such surroundings, to become engulfed and lost in a haze of mystery. People would wonder where she went, but what people, where?

It's because they're not in public anymore that these strangers feel suddenly strange to her, for the first time all night. She reflects on the relative safety she enjoyed before, within the sanctioned confines of spaces that saw all that strangeness distributed equally between them. She registers a growing need to find her way back to that kind of space and starts to wonder which way it is. She sifts through the mush that the alcohol has made of her brain to think about street names, signs, turns. She doesn't know that she's broke yet, but she's thinks she's probably too close to being broke to afford a cab. She musters confidence via the thought that no one will notice if she leaves, because no one here seems to notice much, and slips out through the front door. But she's not even to the end of the block when she hears the footsteps, coming from behind, approaching fast.

"Identity is like a turtle shell out of which the subject keeps craning her/his neck to see if and where it might be possible to move; a way of locating, protecting, masking and disciplining the person." This is the critic Lauren Berlant's gloss on the work Jacques Lacan, a French philosopher who, perhaps more than any other, was interested in investigating the "mirage of stable identity," as Berlant calls it.[5] From Lacan, Berlant grasps the way in which ideas about identity function as support structures but, likewise, as traps for the unsuspecting subject. Identity has the power to shape and thus also to constrict. That is why so much of human life is devoted to a kind of poking at its edges. We seek to discover who we are by locating the boundaries of what we are willing to be.

This is what we see happening in the film *Victoria*. Our main character is unsure of herself from the start: the bartender said no, after all. So when a group of friendly strangers comes along and invites her to join them, it feels like a means of escape from the nagging questions of the self, but also an opportunity for discovery. She follows them up the stairs and out of the club, then down the street, then to the *Späti*, then to the roof of a nearby apartment building, then into a stolen van, then down a ramp to an underground parking garage, then back up out of the garage and to a bank, which the men rob, then back to the same club that denied them entrance where, high on cocaine, they strip off all their clothes and take over the dance floor. The film sets up a series of minor escalations which, on Victoria's part, compel a series of minor, and then increasingly dire, decisions. How much does she trust these strangers? How much does she desire acceptance from them? And to what end?

As the stakes grow higher and the consequences more menacing, we see Victoria "craning her neck to see where it might be possible to move," to recall Berlant. Victoria is not stupid or reckless, she's just lonely. And she's not a bad person, though she participates in events that would surely be judged in that light, in a court of either law or ethics. Outside of these choices, we don't get to know her much as a character, save for in the scene where she gets Sonne alone and confesses that she is in Germany because she has fled a life in which she has been judged unsatisfactory. She was a student at a music conservatory, she tells him, studying piano. She was talented—enough to be accepted there in the first place but not enough, it seems, to progress in her studies and graduate. She was asked to leave and when she did, she left Spain all together. She explains all of this in the darkened café that is now the very ordinary place where she does very ordinary work, the sort that doesn't require any talent at all. On the café's tuneless and battered piano, she plays Liszt's "Mephisto Waltz" and then tells Sonne that she is happy to be there in Berlin, doing her ordinary work. He doesn't see her cry afterward, when she closes the lid of the piano, but the camera does: we do.

In this scene, Victoria admits to being, in essence, undersocialized through her long years of study at the conservatory. This admission provides some rationale for her actions in the film. One gets the sense that she does what she does because she is unsure about what normal socialization ought to entail. That, or maybe she just likes the guys. Maybe she likes Sonne (they kiss there in the darkened café). Maybe she's just having fun hanging out.

Back in Scotland, on that fabled New Year's Eve, I had been mulling some of the same anxious possibilities. I was having fun and so I kept going, kept following the group to the next bar, and the next, and then the house party, and then beyond. When I fled, it was because I had suddenly grown scared. I had thought at first that I was scared of *them*, this amiable group of strangers that seemed to have grown less amiable as the night wore on. But in hindsight, I think it's more likely that I was simply scared of myself and my own powers of decision-making. I had craned my head out of my shell, surveyed my surroundings, and then made a decision. And that decision had landed me in an unknown suburb of a foreign city, without money or resources and without people I could trust, in the company of a group of guys that I had known for only a few hours. I had groped my way in the dark to the boundary line of my own curiosity and discovered something solid and tactile and terrifying there. I couldn't see any way that such a story might end happily for me, so I cut it short, tried to get back to the place where it had last made sense. To the last place where I could remember being me.

Which is why it came as a total surprise to me, the ending, in which nothing whatsoever happened that I didn't want to happen. The steps behind me on the pavement belonged to Mark, who *had* noticed me leaving the party and had come running after me.

Together, we walked back to my friend's apartment with the sun coming up and the streets turning buttery in the light. Later that day, he called the landline at my friend's place to ask me to dinner. It's New Year's Day, everything was closed, so the last time I saw him was over an Indian takeaway, which we shared at my friend's kitchen table.

The last time I heard his voice was several days later when my friend, back from Greece, passed me the phone and told me there was a voice mail for me from "a very nice-sounding young man." It was the night before I was scheduled to leave. The nice young man had called to wish me a safe journey home.

A book that taught me a lot about hanging out and, at the same time, about Scotland is Irvine Welsh's *Trainspotting*. Most people outside of Scotland, if they know it, know it from the film, which is the same as not knowing it at all. Though I appreciate director Danny Boyle's adaptation of Welsh's work, it lacks something—the rapturous use of the Edinburgh variant of the Scots language, for one, but also much of the book's original melancholy. The film, for example, skips over the events of the titular story, "Trainspotting in Leith Central Station," which not only gives the book its name but the whole, larger work so much of its meaning.

Trainspotting is a book about hanging out—with drugs, usually; with friends, often; with strangers, sometimes; and with friends who start to feel or look like strangers, most significantly. This chain of fragile and often fraught relations coalesces in two important scenes involving a certain outsider. The book, which falls somewhere between a novel and a collection of short stories, follows the exploits of a group of friends who live outside Edinburgh.

At the center of that group and posing as its classically toxic alpha male is Begbie. The outsider who appears now and again in the two scenes in question—including in the "Trainspotting" story— is Begbie's father.

This unnamed stranger-father character exerts a haunting influence on Welsh's book. When he does show up, his presence makes for an instant buzzkill that threatens to sabotage the group's fun, which is why his character gets omitted from the film version. It's too sinister an image—one which refracts all the neon colors of the group's carousing and presents them in the muted tones of age and wretchedness. When the group stumbles into the only bar that is open at five o'clock in the morning after a long night of drinking, Begbie's father is there. He forms part of what Welsh describes as a "smattering of the more desperate: the people who are there because they need to be."[6] Begbie's father is an alcoholic and, in many ways, a harbinger of his son's fate. He notices the person who he thinks might be his son, reflecting, "the young man enjoys his company and his drink. He remembers when he himself was in that position. The enjoyment and the company faded away, but the drink didn't. In fact, it expanded to fill in the gap left by their departure."[7] His addiction (like those of his son's friends, most of whom are heroin users), started with hanging out. Eventually, the addiction made hanging out harder, then all but impossible, and then the addiction itself—the company of alcohol—was all that he had left.

Begbie eventually notices the "old drunkard" and ushers the group out of the bar, on to the next stop. But about fifty pages later the two characters meet again, this time in the old Leith Central Station. Unused since the '70s, the station became derelict and thus a hangout for homeless junkies and winos in the 1980s, which is when the action of the book takes place. Begbie's father comes "lurch[ing] up . . . wine boatil in his hand" and introduces the book's catchphrase: "What yis up tae lads? Trainspottin, eh?" He laughs at his own joke; it's a joke because trains haven't run through the station for years, not since the 1950s (the station was converted to a depot for the storage of locomotives in 1956). But what is the meaning of his cryptic use of the word "trainspotting"?

The word refers to a humble pastime that is built on the collecting of experiences—the experience of seeing a particular train going past. It's like a version of the license plate game that bored American children have been known to play on long car rides. The practice began in the UK in the 1930s and '40s, during the era that saw the growth of steam power and the proliferation of steam locomotives. The idea was to stand on a train platform, wait for a locomotive to pass, and record its number, name, and other identifying details. It's another generation's form of hanging out, or playing the *flâneur*, even—a way of doing a minor kind of something that disguises the work of not really doing anything.

When Begbie's father asks Begbie and his friend Mark Renton, who is the book's protagonist, about "trainspottin,'" he is drawing attention to his status as a relic of a bygone era. There are no longer trains to be seen or spotted in Leith Central Station. But there are trainspotters, or people like Begbie's father, still occupying the space, still hanging out. Following this exchange, Renton realizes what he didn't realize fifty pages before, which is that the old man is Begbie's father. Together, he and Begbie leave the old man behind and head down Duke Street, where Begbie mercilessly beats up a stranger. Renton reflects that the guy in question, a "boy," looks at the two of them with "mair . . . resignation than fear" and seems to "underst[and] everything."[8] Which is what, exactly? That he is required to play the victim for Begbie's misdirected anger and, well, daddy issues?

There's so much antisocial behavior in *Trainspotting*, as this scene clearly shows—so many impediments to camaraderie and hanging out. Though the novel is occasionally tender, portraying great intimacy between the members of the main crew, those moments are often punctured or cut short by scenes of violence and conflict, with Begbie usually serving as a prime instigator. In fact, he ends up playing the same role that heroin does in their hanging out. He facilitates sociality as much as he corrodes it, steering all that intimacy off course. Thus, while *Trainspotting* is not quite a book about hanging out with strangers, it muses on a related set of circumstances: it's about not knowing when or how to stop hanging out with friends or people or things that are killing you.

In the film *Victoria*, the only time the camera stops moving is at the very end, when Victoria has, at last, ceased hanging out with people and things that are killing her, or at least threatening to kill her. After a final, explosive scene that takes place in an upscale hotel in downtown Berlin, Victoria leaves by herself. She has returned to the state of aloneness in which she started the film but, as the viewer now sees, it is very much for her own good. The camera, which has been relentlessly circling her for the past two hours, finally pauses in its tracks and grows still. It continues to film her as she walks away, but it does not follow: it allows her to grow smaller and smaller, to fade into the haze that fills the early-morning streets of Mitte, and then to finally disappear altogether. Victoria has escaped the peril of hanging out with strangers, but she is alone again and the viewer is left to wonder what will become of her, if she will ever summon the courage to repeat the experiment.

Back in Scotland all those years ago, I could have been Victoria, but I wasn't. I enjoyed the night that I spent with the rambunctious group of oil rig workers, strangers though they were; and afterward, I enjoyed the extra day and a half that I spent in Mark's company. In both cases, there was a feeling of freedom that came from knowing that our relations had a kind of logistical shelf life and, even better, little chance of surviving beyond it. Even at that young age, I had already been too much hurt by my own insistence on keeping things alive that maybe didn't deserve to be—things that weren't strong enough to survive via such inconsistent and haphazard propagation. A night with strangers taught me that it can still be good, even if it has to end. Sometimes especially if it has to end.

Recently, during the fall of 2021, I was in Berlin, doing some more hanging out with strangers though, this time, those strangers were simply colleagues I had never met in person before. I went in feeling like I sort of knew them and came away feeling like I knew them a little bit more, if not enough to call them friends. On one evening during that trip, Dave and I were in Mitte and had some time to kill before dinner. We stopped into the bar of the Westin hotel on Friedrichstraße, a fabled strip of street that the German writer Robert Walser describes as being "polished by human destinies."[9] I didn't know that it was the same hotel, the one in which the final scene of *Victoria* takes place, the place she turns her back on as she walks away at the end of the film. But once inside, I knew it immediately, I recognized it.

I mentioned this in passing the next night, to one of those colleagues. He and I had met for coffee and then the coffee turned, at his suggestion, into glasses of warm, milky absinthe. I mentioned that I had accidentally wound up in the lobby of a hotel I recognized from a movie I couldn't stop thinking about, without really knowing why I was mentioning it, and then felt myself tumbling into a description of plans for a book about hanging out, one I didn't even know I was writing yet. I felt then a sort of through line running between my impressions of the film *Victoria*, my memories of traveling alone and hanging out with strangers, and skipping from coffee to an all-absinthe bar with this colleague, effectively also a stranger to me. In all three instances there was that thrill of incongruity, of chance, and lurking just beneath it, a flash of that old feeling of *peril*, scraping away at the inside of my stomach.

"Traveling inspires camaraderie," says Walser, and he doesn't say why.[10] But I know why. It's because, as age takes hold and actions become calcified, the opportunities for that exhilarating, perilous strangeness grow fewer. We become used to things, including ourselves. We settle for more polite and ritualized approaches to hanging out.

The company of strangers has the power to upset all of this and to put us back on edge. It forces us to reckon with the idea that whatever happens next, for once, it won't be what we planned on.

3

JAMMING AS HANGING OUT

Like almost everyone I knew back then, I spent my twenties playing music in bands. In Pittsburgh, I played in two. One of them was good. The other was popular.

The good one worked hard at being good. It formed slowly over the course of a decade, gathering within its grasp a number of first-rate musicians—players of varying ages who knew the ins and outs of their instruments, knew their histories and capabilities. In that band, we spoke a shared language of keys and scales and modes. There were time signatures and tempos, transitions and changes, harmonics and dynamics. This was a band where we all carried little notebooks full of staff paper so we could write our parts out, note by note. We were forever revisiting and tinkering with yesterday's decisions, trying to improve upon them, to bring them up to a place where they could rest and ripen. We knew and riffed off of the greats, measuring ourselves against them. We made some albums. We played some shows. We broke up once a year, every year, from the pressure that was mostly our own invention, and then got back together again. We were good. We were not popular.

The other band was a different beast, made up of young amateurs who were more interested in the work of figuring out how to creatively exist together, I think, than in perfecting and exhibiting their skills as musicians. In that band, I was the only one who read music. Instead of notebooks full of staff paper, we carried thirty-racks or bottles or joints to share. Rehearsals were as much about talking and telling stories as they were about learning or getting our hands around new songs. We spoke the folk vernacular of numbered chords. We made and swapped audio recordings with each other, building up a song from its individual parts, and then immediately started improvising on whatever it was we had already mapped out. We were not good, but we were enthusiastic about being together. That enthusiasm proved to be of a viral sort, capable of infecting whole rooms. We headlined sold-out concerts. We hooked up with a local record label. We counted the city's mayor as a loyal fan. We toured. We hung out.

That more popular band was called The Armadillos, not a name I would have chosen for them had I been around in the early days of the group and allowed to decide, which I was not. The name served us, though, because it was nondescript and left enough space for growth in its vagueness. Though we always played the same type of music, we would use different words to describe it depending on the day, venue, audience, and mood. Sometimes we were a punk band, sometimes a country band. Sometimes we made a lot of noise and slipped in a Clash cover or two; sometimes we played all-acoustic and made only a little noise, with a few splashes of Gram Parsons thrown in.

I found my way into the band because I answered an ad for a fiddler. I didn't play the fiddle, I played the accordion, and I talked the others in the band into believing that this was what they really wanted. I played my accordion so much back then, because of The Armadillos, that, to this day, strapping myself into my instrument

feels like arriving back home after a journey of Odyssean proportions. Its bellows exude an everyday smell that I once knew back in
another, fabled time.

I owe much of what I've come to know about hanging out to
both of my Pittsburgh bands, but especially to The Armadillos. It
was with them that I gained, or perhaps gave myself, permission to
revel in the kind of shared quest for meaning that is the privileged
domain of youth. In the other band, the good band, I was the young-
est. Everyone else in it had jobs and homes and kids and responsibilities. But with The Armadillos, it was different. If we had jobs, we
hated and were trying to quit them. Our homes, meanwhile, were
marked by similar conditions of contingency: they came and went,
evaporating at the end of a lease or due to a sudden rise in the rent
and, in some cases, proved even temporarily nonexistent.

One of the guys in the band, Matt, spent a year living in a
squat—an old, abandoned rowhouse on the city's North Side that
had no electricity and no functional plumbing, where residents
came and went and showers were decanted from a rain barrel
on the roof. Back then, the band practiced wherever we could
manage to and sometimes that meant practicing at the squat. But
there were obstacles to be found there: too many people and, in
the wintertime, not enough heat (none, in fact, save for a wood-
stove in the kitchen).

Sometimes we practiced at my place. At the time, the place
in question was a duplex that I shared with my boyfriend. It was
located on the edge of Pittsburgh's Little Italy neighborhood and we
had the upstairs. The downstairs neighbors already hated us and we
hated them, so having the band over didn't pose additional threats
to that existing situation.

Sometimes, though, we would practice at Austin's place—when the band had a gig on the South Side, or when he couldn't get access to the car he shared with his girlfriend. Austin was the lead singer and lead guitarist, the guy who started the band, and he lived on the Slopes, as they are known, in an apartment building that, each day, seemed to slide closer to the mouth of a dark, trash-infested canyon. In this way, it was like many houses located in the more affordable parts of Pittsburgh, tucked into and occupying a seam of shadow and imminent disaster.

Austin's place had its own challenges. The biggest was his downstairs neighbor, a man of indeterminately advanced age who was also a heavy drinker. Depending on the time of day, the guy downstairs might be found home and asleep, home and drunk, or gone at his restaurant job. The problem had to do with the inconsistency of these states. We never knew when he might be home and we were too afraid of him to investigate fully. The first several times I practiced with the band at Austin's, it ended early, with his neighbor pounding on the ceiling and threatening to call the cops.

One day, though, it was different: we caught him in another mood, on his way up instead of down, maybe. We were rehearsing a song on which I sang lead and the guy came barreling up the stairs. Austin, anticipating a confrontation, winced as he opened the door, only to find his neighbor standing there, trembling, amidst the darkness of the wood-paneled hallway. His face was pale and shining—wet, actually—and his body vibrated not with aggression but, rather, vulnerability.

"That voice, that voice, that's . . . *Irish*," he said. He was gesturing to me and something about the way he said the word "Irish" made it sound like a euphemism for a word he couldn't quite bring himself to say, or else one that had become lost to him over the years. "It reminds me . . . it reminds me . . ." But then he couldn't get the rest of it out, whatever it was.

He left abruptly—back to his own apartment, we thought—but then returned some moments later with a case of Keystone from the corner store, a gift for the band. He wanted to hang out. He wanted to listen to us play some more. He wanted us to do a song he liked, "The Old Triangle," a sappy one that I knew from hanging around the local sessions. We felt our way through its chords, obligingly, for his sake, as we drank the proffered beer.

After that, we thought things would be different, better between all of us. But then, the next time, it was like all the other times before and our playing couldn't do anything to pacify him. He was back to banging on the ceiling and screaming obscenities—caught at different, perhaps more painful points along the arc of his own inner pendulum, and hellbent on shutting us down.

What made The Armadillos so different from the other band, the good band, was what I have come to understand as a spirit of accessibility and ease. We played to hang out, to "jam," as musicians have insisted on calling it now for generations. Where the other band worked to collectively polish its songs until they shone without streaks, making them fit for performance, The Armadillos were content to simply let things casually unspool. What resulted was the opposite of professionalism. It was, instead, something endearingly ragged—a rough assemblage, a momentary convergence.

I've never liked the word, *jam*, and yet I find there is no worthy substitute for it. *Jam* may refer to a whole combination of activities, but central to them is a collaborative space—both literal and figurative—in which music is given the chance to unfurl in loose, rambling, and unceremonious ways. The space of the jam is, crucially, one that exists outside of the formal rituals of performance. To jam is to explore, improvise, swap, share, and relate. That process is a fundamentally messy one, often filled with what would, under the auspices of traditional performance, be deemed mistakes. You can hear all of this in the word itself, *jam*, which, being an onomatopoeia, seems to sonically describe a situation of convergence. It's a little, three-letter wreck of a word, containing the sounds of twisted metal and broken glass.

The poet Hayden Carruth, at least, sees it in this way. There are those, he concedes, who associate the word with something sticky and delicious, "like blackberry preserves on your bagel . . . [but] I think it means something more like a traffic jam . . . Indeed the jargon of jazz is full of threatening and abusive terms, just as it is full of innuendo."[1] I take Carruth's point about the traffic jam, even as I ignore his interest in the word's more stereotypically masculine connotations involving violence. Because in my experience, this is not how jamming works: it's not about violence, competition, or muscling into the music, though it may appear that way on the surface. Rather, to jam is to hold a space open for the exploration of that kind of chaotic convergence, to listen and see if the things that feel at first like mistakes might, in the end, light the way toward new opportunities. To jam means to occupy the here and now, to take up residence within the error-filled instance, and to do this in the presence of others who are content to do the same.

The problem with the jam—call it the practice, the rehearsal—is, often, the guy downstairs. Carruth names this very problem in an essay from the 1980s. He relates some of his own experiences playing in and around Chicago during the post-war era in the company of a pianist named Don Ewell, a talented musician who, despite all his skill, was built for the jam, not the stage. As Carruth explains, Ewell's "personality was not suited to playing in public or, even worse, into a microphone."[2] Carruth then goes on to describe how their private musical collaborations were often stymied by a familiar foe.

> Sometimes when I was there I'd unsling my clarinet and we'd play together: that is, we'd try to. Almost always after about eight bars the guy downstairs would start hammering on his ceiling with a broom handle. Sometimes he did it so quickly it seemed as if he must have been waiting there for us to begin. We called him every kind of squarehead and Philistine we could think of. Mostly we called him an asshole.[3]

Any musician living in an urban area stands to make as many enemies as friends through their music. That is the flip side of the jam which, through its noise, has the power to gather together and assemble but also the power to offend and alienate. And, because the noise that results from the jam can be intrusive, seeping into the lives of others, it also has the power to provoke.

This is a power that is somewhat unique to the jam because of the way that it is made to happen outside of consecrated performance spaces. No one faults a musician for making a lot of noise inside a concert hall or a padded practice room. But the jam does not, cannot thrive inside those spaces. It requires basements or kitchens, park benches or lawns, or else grubby corners of public drinking establishments. It requires, in other words, social adjacency. And because of that adjacency and its reliance on it, its mess cannot be contained.

This is the case even when jamming happens in perceived isolation, through solo practice. Amit Chaudhuri, a novelist and also a musician trained in the classical Indian tradition, relates his own experiences with the guy downstairs in his luminous memoir *Finding the Raga*. Chaudhuri's guy downstairs lives in London and instead of downstairs, he's upstairs, actually. But as with all guys of this sort, this neighbor is quick to communicate his annoyance via "stirrings [from] above, disgruntled, incoherent, each heavy footfall a protest." The result is three years spent in what Chaudhuri calls "a state of siege."[4]

After Dave and I lost our duplex apartment, the one where the guys downstairs made enough of their own noise to deserve what they got from us upstairs, we relocated to a rowhouse apartment in Pittsburgh's Mexican War Streets neighborhood. That is where I came to know my own state of siege. As with Chaudhuri, whose neighbors weaponized their stereo systems in retribution for the noise generated by his practice, my siege was waged on two fronts. We shared a wall with a rowdy Irish bar that would spill its guts, in the form of screaming human contents, out onto the street every night at closing time. Meanwhile, on the other side of us lived a woman who played her kitchen wall like a drum whenever the band would convene for practice. I resented the noise of the drunks outside my window as much as I fought to protect my own right to jam, to make noise, within the space of my apartment and among my chosen circle of noisemakers.

Because we had to practice, of course, we had to jam. Without that preparatory, exploratory work, the stuff we did onstage, into microphones, was fated to falter. This is in spite of the fact that, as a band, much of our success came from making the work of performance look relaxed and accessible, as opposed to planned. There was an organic quality to the way we made music together onstage, but all of that ease had to be forged through the mess of the jam. We had to get good and be good with each other in order to get good at being good *in front of* others. This was true on a social level as much as it was on a musical one. In both cases, we were working to set a foundation in private that might evolve to support the weight of our creative improvisation in public.

The concept of improvisation is one that appears nested inside that of jamming. Derek Bailey, author of one the foundational treatises on the theory of improvisation, laments the way in which the term gets misused. As he sees it, there's a tendency to treat improvisation as a sobriquet for anti-preparation, as "a completely ad hoc activity, frivolous and inconsequential, lacking in design and method."[5] Bailey, though, argues that the opposite is actually true: improvisation, he says, is really only made possible thanks to preparation and training. A player has to get comfortable with their skills in order to let loose and truly improvise. Thus improvisation itself is backed by its apparent opposite, practice—lots of it. The trick is to take all that practice and iron it smooth in the moment of presentation.

The Armadillos never got famous. Fame wasn't even part of the equation for us. We didn't allow ourselves to dream of it because to do so would have meant chasing after impossible things, unicorns and dragons and the like. We arrived too late in this world for the kind of fame that once sustained artists and musicians, allowing them to stitch together passable, if passing, careers from the multi-colored scraps of audience appreciation—record deals, album sales, and years of incessant gigging. Likewise, we arrived too early for the Spotify takeover of all that was music and for the kind of fame that, today, spreads chiefly through social media without ever yield-ing enough to keep a band in beer and guitar strings, even.

On the last album we recorded together, before we parted ways in 2014, there's a song that gets at this idea—swipes at it in broad, nebulous ways. Austin wrote it. It's one of his best, composed at a time when he had started to feel like he was out of ideas, out of songs, and out of energy for the continuous fight that was required to keep making them. Though we would proceed to put it this song of his on an album and play it live in dozens of shows over the course of two more years, I remember hearing in it a kind of musical fare-well to the world we had built together. As he was writing it, he came to me for help with the chorus and I had to tell him that it didn't need one, it was already perfect. At the culmination of all the verses of the song, which is called "Times New Roman," is a simple statement: "I thought we were living in a different time."

To this day, I can't decide if this is true, if we really thought this, though I'm certain that we felt it. In many ways, we had never had a choice when it came to confronting the realities of our time. Our activities as a band had begun in the winter of 2009. They became the light and heat around which the four of us huddled, there in the shadows of the 2008 recession. We felt ourselves to be living in a sort of generational ditch that no amount of talent or success could break us out of, so we concentrated on having fun together, instead. If we didn't think we were living in a different time, we at least felt a desire to believe in such delusions and in our right to entertain them.

We weren't famous, but we were popular, at least in a limited, local sense. That meant we had connections. We hosted bands when they came through town and then asked and received the same favors, in turn. Each summer, we toured south to Asheville, North Carolina—Big Rock Candy Mountain as we called it. There, you could sleep out every night, if it was summer and if you had to, and the handouts really did appear to grow on bushes, just like in the song. In Asheville, an hour's worth of busking usually got us a full tank of gas, plus a round of burritos and beers on the side. We were friendly with another band that was based there. Its three members lived in a tiny rented house that sat jacked up on stilts and fronting the Swannanoa River. It was one in a line of identical houses, all of them similarly filled with musicians and bandmates. It was a whole neighborhood of splashy, summery, musical mayhem, without a single guy downstairs in sight.

What drew us, time and again, to the Asheville scene was the fact that our friends could manage to make it there as full-time musicians—well, nearly full-time. They all did odd jobs to fill in the cracks in their respective incomes, but only the ones that left them ample time for jamming. One of those jobs involved capping and labeling bottles of beer for a local microbrewery, which they all did together one night a week. They were paid by the case and then also allowed to take extra beer home with them.

One July night, when The Armadillos were staying with them, our friends went off to cap and label bottles as usual and we stayed back at the house on stilts. It had a big communal yard that ran down to the river and in the middle of it was a fire ring surrounded by stumps that had been positioned for use as seating. We got the fire going, took out our instruments, and started trading songs and jamming. We did a lot of this type of thing while on tour; it was a way to productively dispense with all the downtime, of which there was always plenty to be found. As we played there around the fire, the dark descended upon us, wiping out the surrounding scenery and replacing it with deep blue shadows. Out of these shadows emerged a guy with a guitar, his face barely visible in the firelight. He wasn't one of the neighbors and we'd never seen him before. Without a word of greeting, he sat down and just started playing along, inserting himself within whatever song we already had going. A few minutes later, a woman with a fiddle followed, then another guy with another guitar. Then a djembe. Then a banjo.

On it went. We'd seen no cars approach and had no idea where they came from, these improvisatory ghosts. They sprang up out of the night, armed with a knowledge of our chords and our songs or, at least, enough skill to quickly piece it all together and join right in. I played a Gillian Welch song. The woman with the fiddle asked if I knew any more. I started in on "Red Clay Halo" and she was ready with a complementary fiddle part and also vocal harmonies on the chorus. It was fluid and easy, like a conversation between old friends. It was hanging out—delighting in a shared project, a shared language, with no guys downstairs and no one listening in from the outside, badgering us with requests or demanding a sculpted, polished performance. There was *no* performance. There was just us, a group of strangers, all gathered together in the dark, listening to each other.

Later, we learned the truth of the serendipitous occurrence. One of the neighbors had been trying to inaugurate a weekly jam session and had been advertising it locally. But then, apparently, he forgot all about the date he'd set and went off to make some money capping bottles along with the rest. The strangers emerging out of the darkness had seen the fire and been drawn to it and then, upon encountering us, had assumed one of us was him, the guy who had put the jam session together. They didn't ask clarifying questions and neither did we, since answers weren't required for participation. All that was required was tuning up and hanging out.

Some parts of touring were hard, but Asheville was always easy. That's why we made it a sort of locus of our wanderings south. Our tour itineraries would have us return there, looping like barn swallows, every couple of days. It was our refuge. No matter how the audiences treated us in Johnson City, Athens, Chapel Hill, Wilmington, or Greenville, Asheville was there to take us in. It gave to us reliably in the form of funds—there was always money to be earned from busking or "sitting in," as it is called, on someone else's gig—and it also had the advantage of reliable shelter. If the weather was bad and our tents were still wet from the night before, we knew we could always camp out on our friends' living room floor.

But Asheville also gave to us, I think, in the form of lessons in humility. There, it seemed like everyone was a musician, and every band we met was better than our own. They all had talent, they were all going places, without signaling so much as the desire to even leave town.

It was in Asheville that I encountered one of my own musical heroes, and in surprisingly humble surroundings. I had come of age as a teen in the 1990s, which meant, for a traditional instrumentalist, being raised on a diet of musical influences that came courtesy of the '90s Celtic revival. (For those of you who missed it, it started with *Riverdance* in 1995 and petered out about a decade later, along with the fortunes of the many talented musicians who had been content to play their instruments in relative obscurity before they were ever lifted up on its passing tide.) One of the revival's stars was a guitarist named John Doyle, a founding member of the group Solas, a band of distressingly epic talents and one of the best to ever make it mildly big during that era. If anything, Solas had too much talent—they were weighed down by it and also by the personalities that came with it. They had formed as a sort of Celtic supergroup and almost as quickly as they arrived, they began to splinter. That splintering followed quick on the heels of their modest celebrity, which, in 1990s trad music terms, involved winning a Grammy in one of those categories that they don't show on television, plus some appearances on *A Prairie Home Companion*.

John Doyle's playing—jazz-inflected, layered, and exquisitely dexterous—had always been the bedrock of the band, at least to my ears. He left the group around 2000 and embarked on a mostly solo career that was to be rooted in Asheville. Which is where I found him on a random Monday night in the middle of July, playing backup for a contra dance.

A contra dance, by the way, is like a square dance except it tilts Celtic where a square dance tilts country. Live contra dances usually feature backing bands made up of guitar, fiddle, and sometimes other instruments like concertina, mandolin, or bouzouki. I'd heard that Doyle was something of a fixture in the Asheville scene, but I hadn't expected to discover him in such a context. But I should have. The sort of fame that attaches itself to idiosyncratic talents, like being the best Celtic guitarist on the planet, is humble. It does not set boundaries for itself; it simply moves from point to point along a chain of plausible opportunities. I don't know if he was a regular in the contra dance group or if he was simply sitting in, but he was there, head bent toward his guitar, and playing as well as I'd ever heard him on any recording.

Later, back home in Pittsburgh, I'd gush to the other band, the good band, about seeing him live and they would be jealous and impressed. But to The Armadillos, as to most people in the room that night, he and his talents were just a backdrop, there to support and enliven what was, essentially, a social gathering—a time and a place to hang out.

Improvisation is one of the central threads that ties jamming to hanging out. Both grow from the seed of an initial, improvised act, from which there forms a halo—a gathering storm of creative invention, if you will. Dan DiPiero, a music historian, groups the two together under the heading of "contingency," observing that "in both musical and social situations, improvisation is itself a contingent activity that necessarily emerges in response to and as a part of contingent situations."[6] Which is to say, we are all just making it up as we go along and improvisation is something that certain musical and social situations do not invent but, rather, help to make explicit. In jamming, as in hanging out, there are few, if any, real rules. Sure, there are key signatures and tempos, which function sort of like guardrails: they keep a player in their lane but, when necessary, can also be overcome, dispensed with and then, sometimes, returned to. But there are no strict rules about what one has to play or how they have to play it. There is no fidelity, in other words, to a given standard, except for those that are socially constructed on the fly by the jam session's participants. Standards exist for the enforcement of comfort and jamming is about discovering fertile ground for its opposite.

I said before that jamming with those mystery musicians in Asheville was like conversation, like talking. This is because, though we were strangers and hadn't met before, we already spoke the same language, to the point of being able to comfortably improvise and embellish upon each other's uses of it. This is Fred Moten's way of viewing improvisation which, he says, "is located at a seemingly unbridgeable chasm between feeling and reflection, disarmament and preparation, speech and writing." The "speech" of improvisation is immediate and ad hoc, while the "writing" of improvisation involves laying something down that can be returned to later. It is this combination that leads Moten to call improvisation "speech *without foresight*."[7] It lacks foresight because it cannot see what is coming and so is driven to constantly adapt and make use of whatever is there, even as it is still arriving. But there's an undeniable element of futurity—Moten calls it "prophecy"—that arises from such processes. To improvise is to anticipate and plan without working toward a definite outcome. It's a form of prophecy without pronouncement, a way of imagining the future without committing to the limitations of what that future has to be.

In his classic short story "Sonny's Blues," the author James Baldwin takes up these themes of uncertainty and prophecy. He couches them, in symbolic terms, within the world of improvisational jazz but then spins a story that is about much more than just jazz. It centers on two brothers who differ in their visions of what the future should look like. "I'm thinking about my future . . . I think about it all the time," the character Sonny tells his brother, who is Baldwin's unnamed narrator. It's a response to a searching admonishment. The narrator doesn't believe that Sonny, who has aspirations of becoming a jazz musician, is serious. He still sees his kid brother as just that, as a kid, meaning someone who can't be trusted not to squander whatever is given to him. He also worries that Sonny, as a musician, is not good enough to make it. "You're getting to be a big boy," he warns him, ". . . it's time you started thinking about your future."[8]

Not *the* future—not what happens the day after tomorrow. *Your* future, the story that hasn't been told yet that nevertheless has you in it.

A main source of conflict in this story stems from Sonny's struggles to explain his ambitions to his comparatively more sensible and grounded brother. Unlike Sonny, Baldwin's narrator has chosen his future already: it involves teaching algebra to high school kids. He does this job without enthusiasm but, instead, with the conviction that what he's doing is *right*, that it makes sense, that it is reasonable. Somewhere in the middle of the story, though, the narrator's young daughter dies. It's a tragedy that is only mentioned in passing, but it gives renewed weight to a set of nagging questions. It forces the narrator to wonder: if it was really stability that he was choosing all along and life has proven itself to be nonetheless unstable, what was the point of choosing that stability in the first place?

These questions help to focus attention on the narrator's brother's ambitions. Sonny explains that playing jazz is "the only thing" he wants to do[9]—the only thing that excites and compels him enough to keep him away from more destructive forces, namely heroin. His brother is opposed to the idea because it's an incomprehensible one to him. To commit to playing jazz would be to commit to a whole life of improvisation, not just in musical terms but in the larger terms of employment and futurity. The narrator wants to be able to rest knowing that his younger brother, who already has a criminal record and drug conviction under his belt at age seventeen, is safe. He does not want to suffer through years of watching Sonny improvise his way through the world.

I love this story and, in my work as an English professor, I teach it often, usually to college freshmen. It's a story that brims with pain and complication: there is the narrator's love for Sonny and also the narrator's selfish wish to see Sonny make safer decisions—more like the ones he has made for himself, which he secretly despises. But, at the same time, there is the narrator's dawning awareness that it is only through risk that one is able to glimpse and have a chance at discovering true reward. He wants Sonny to be happy and he wants for himself to be happy in knowing that Sonny is secure, and he understands that these two outcomes are utterly irreconcilable.

Of course, for Baldwin's characters, the conditions of vulnerability that make Sonny's improvisatory approach to life all the more dangerous are furthermore compounded by racism. Baldwin's characters are Black and they are living in post-war Harlem, amidst a largely Black milieu, but this does not mean they are safe. By way of comparison, the narrator reflects on the hazards that defined his grandparents' and parents' upbringing in the South, which included threats of lynching and, in the case of one family member, murder. This is his way of explaining that he and Sonny live in New York because their ancestors were forced to flee racially motivated violence in the Jim Crow–era South, which marks them as products of the Great Migration. That term refers to the historical relocation of roughly six million African Americans between 1910 and 1970. The Great Migration brought Black artistic talent to northern cities like New York and Chicago. Indeed, Hayden

Carruth (who was white), when he writes of jamming around Chicago in the 1940s in the presence of Black musicians, is talking about the Great Migration—talking about benefiting from, and inserting himself within, an artistic wellspring that was born from conditions of violence and intimidation. That's not how he puts it, of course, but that's the historical context that subtends everything he has to say about jazz and, likewise, everything Baldwin has to say about it in "Sonny's Blues."

At the end of Baldwin's story, the narrator agrees to attend a performance of Sonny's jazz band. In that new setting, he is forced to see his brother—and his brother's art—differently. He finds himself positioned outside "Sonny's world," as he calls it, which is the insular world of the jam. He cannot enter into it. He can only watch from beyond and glean information about it from the bits that leak out or get tossed his way. What he sees in them at first looks like a struggle: Sonny plays the piano as though engaging in combat. "He and the piano stammered, started one way, got scared, stopped; started another way, panicked, marked time, started again; then seemed to have found a direction, panicked again, got stuck." Yet after this, when the band moves onto a different song, Sonny appears to relax into the jam and then everything changes. "Sonny began to play. Something began to happen . . . Then they all came together again, and Sonny was part of the family again. I could tell this from his face. He seemed to have found, right there beneath his fingers, a damn brand-new piano."[10]

The narrator sees his brother as a critical part of a larger machine, rather than as a lone operative who courts danger through reckless actions. He witnesses Sonny's transformation within the improvisatory context of the jam. And that moment teaches him something his brother could not. He releases his grip and gives his brother over to the experience of the error-filled instance, as I called it previously. "I was yet aware that this was only a moment," the narrator reflects, "that the world waited outside, as hungry as a tiger, and that trouble stretched above us, longer than the sky."[11] But, for the time being, Sonny has made a home for himself inside a loose circle of temporary inclusion, of care. It is as good as any that he, as his older brother, might have made for him, and so he leaves him to it, sensing that he has neither the right nor the power to insist on any substitutes.

The space of the jam is always temporary, but its significance is never diminished by that quality. Indeed, if anything, it is heightened via the promise of reoccurrence. The jam, unlike the performance, has no true beginning and thus no end. It lives in the middle for as long as it is allowed to and then it goes dormant, awaiting its opportunity to live again somewhere else. This is also what keeps it from being commodified: when you buy a ticket to a concert, that ticket promises the delivery of something resembling a finished product. But a jam, in being essentially always unfinished, cannot be bought and sold in the same way. It resists commodification in existing for its own ends, rather than as a means to better, more valuable ones.

Back in my Pittsburgh days, I became friendly with a group of people who I referred to as my "old man jam band," and it was through them that I received critical training in the art of improvisation. My label for this group does not do them justice. They weren't that old, or at least, they didn't act like it when they were playing their instruments, though it's true that most of them had forty or more years on me. And they weren't all men. They weren't even really a band, not in a formal sense, because there were always others like me, haunting the fringes and sitting in. This prevented the group from taking solid shape as a band, which I think they rather liked. They had a name, which they used for logistical purposes and for booking performances, but those performances were like loose extensions of their jam sessions, with the contents simply turned inside out. As performers, they were utterly guileless, likely to deliver the exact same show inside an amphitheater as they would inside somebody's living room.

The first time I ever played with them, it was at the Benedum, a massive art deco theater located in downtown Pittsburgh and usually reserved for performances by the Pittsburgh Symphony Orchestra. Frank Sinatra used to perform there and Bob Marley gave his last concert there. The old man jam band had been hired as the opening act for the movie *Gasland*, which was touring at the time along with its writer and director Josh Fox, himself a banjo player. The group did not rehearse ahead of time and I was given no preparation in the form of setlists or the like. I simply showed up with my accordion, did a quick mic check, and was asked which songs I would like to play and in which keys. I was terrified—unnecessarily, since everything went fine, of course.

From this experience I formed lasting friendships with many of the group's core members, especially with a banjo and guitar player named Tom. A descendent of the Pete Seeger school of both social justice and musical jamming, Tom's philosophy holds that anything can be learned and, until it is learned, it can at least be improvised. It's this outlook, I think, that gives his playing a feeling of such exploratory fearlessness. When I started jamming with Tom, it seemed that he had lived everywhere and knew every song. Now, more than a decade later, I know most of the ones he knows and I have him to thank for that knowledge.

I learned these songs from Tom under a wide range of conditions and within a wide range of settings. I learned them while we crouched by the fading campfire that was our only light on a sweltering July night, somewhere along a backpacking trail that traces the West Virginia border. I learned them in my neighbor's backyard in the Mexican War Streets, which I once commandeered for an outdoor session when it became apparent that she wasn't home. I learned them in Tom's dining room, or else in his car, on the way to a gig we were supposed to be playing together (a wedding, no less). I learned them from the stack of mix CDs he made to get me all the way from Pennsylvania, my old home, to my new one in North Dakota, amidst a torrent of tears that lasted me all the way to Cleveland. And I learned some of them all over again, recently, when he came to visit me in Vermont. Together, we jammed until the early hours of the morning, like I didn't have classes to teach the next morning, like time didn't exist, and like seven years hadn't elapsed since the last time life had allowed us to do it.

"I love that song," Tom kept saying as he paused to swap his banjo for his guitar or vice versa. "Nobody plays that song anymore. How do *you* know that song?"

"I learned it from you, Tom," I kept telling him.

As much as jamming is about improvisation, it also about education. My years of jamming with Tom and others like him have rested upon an invisible scaffold formed from listening and learning. The same, I want to argue, is true where hanging out is concerned: being with someone, or with a whole group of someones, and transforming that act of being into something that is worthwhile and meaningful, requires listening but also assiduous digestion—the thoughtful processing of whatever one has heard. That kind of digestion gets easier over time, through repeated exposure. The knowledge base that is fed from each successive instance grows more solid so that, after a while, improvisation feels like a more stable enterprise, less threatening and less risky.

But all of this takes years. It cannot be forced into instant formation, over the course of a few interactions.

This is how we get from improvisation, which is a species of spontaneous activity, to study, which is a more concentrated and programmatic one. *Study* is the word Fred Moten uses to get at the idea of repeated exposure to a concept, a practice, or a particular way of being. Folded into the work of study are all manner of activities relating to preparation: planning, consideration, learning, repetition, reinforcement, and memory. One pursues these activities in order to plan ahead for the work of improvising in the moment and in order to make that work, which is always uncomfortable, a little bit less so. For Moten and his longtime intellectual collaborator, Stefano Harney, the work of study is located right next door to that of hanging out:

> It's talking and walking around with other people, working, dancing, suffering, some irreducible convergence of all three, held under the name of speculative practice. The notion of a rehearsal—being in a kind of workshop, playing in a band, in a jam session, or old men sitting on a porch, or people working together in a factory—there are these

various modes of activity. The point of calling it "study" is
to mark that the incessant and irreversible intellectuality of
these activities is already present.[12]

It's that incessantness, which gets expressed as habit and compulsion,
that draws me to this comment of Moten's, and likewise to the connection he makes here between study and jamming. The former, we
are often told, is supposed to be serious, while the other is supposed
to be about play. Yet, in Moten's view, where they meet is within that
middle ground that is the site of "incessant" return, of learning.

Carruth, too, talks about returning to the site of the jam, which
is less a location than a social context. At the end of his essay "The
Guy Downstairs," he describes what happened several decades later,
in the 1970s, well after both he and his friend Don Ewell had left
Chicago. The two kept in touch and, on a few occasions, Ewell came
to visit him at his home in Vermont, a place that I now have in common with Carruth and a place to which I now find myself luring
old friends, like Tom, for the sake of jamming. Carruth explains
that Ewell had by then suffered a stroke that left one arm paralyzed.
"Nevertheless he was playing well, and still with the same devotion
of earlier years," Carruth writes. This consoling thought stands in
contrast to the end of the essay, in which Carruth grieves not just the
death of Ewell, who he fears may be dead by the time of his writing
it, but a whole class of people like him—those driven, like Baldwin's
Sonny, to improvise their ways through life. Carruth finishes out the
essay with a dour observation: those pursuers of "ecstatic freedom"
have conceded and "the guy downstairs has taken over the world."[13]

It's Carruth's way of saying that the bad guys have won, but I
refuse to believe it. When I moved to North Dakota, away from

my friend Tom and the whole old man jam band (who I still miss dearly), I didn't leave them behind. I took them with me in the form of knowledge and song. Two thousand miles later, I took to jamming with a young man named Michael, a student of mine with a devastating gift for all things string-related. Now he plays with a big-time Chicago-based bluegrass outfit, through which, though he likely doesn't know it, he is continuing to scatter little bits of my old friends' influences. The point is that the jam, unlike the performance, lives on, even when it leaves our hands, and even when we no longer find ourselves able to be a part of it.

The Armadillos were popular, but our recordings were not. We were never happy with the albums we made. We struggled to translate the live energy of our shows to the arid confines of MP3 files, the designated vessels for our music's preservation and commodification. I think these struggles arose in large part from the recording process itself.

Modern audio recording is all about the *track*, meaning an individual player's or singer's individual sound that is individually captured and then, through the magic of mixing, blended together with all the other individual tracks made by all the other individual players. It's an extremely lonely process, one that drains the live jam of its collaborative qualities. In place of a band, or a group of people, what you have with track recording is the pure isolation of the individual player, who gets corralled into a soundproof booth and then strapped into a set of headphones. The headphones become the player's only link back to the memory of a more gratifying collaborative process. They also play the role of taskmaster: the headphones relay a *base track*—usually guitar—that is meant to keep the player in line. The player listens to this track and then they listen to themselves recording their part along with it. Sometimes, if things get too messy and start to run off course, the audio engineer will add in a truly loathsome thing, a *click track*, that bashes the players eardrums with the punishing force of a metronome.

The word *track* is itself indicative of how this whole process is supposed to work. Where jamming presents opportunities for convergence and redirection, track recording offers only a narrow channel and then demands that the player fit their music inside of it. Running alongside that channel are others just like it, made by other musicians, but the player cannot see or hear them. The historical event of the jam, the instance that inspired all the music in the first place, gets erased.

Today, audio engineers and sound professionals rely on track recording because of its convenience. It's easier to capture one track at a time and then mix them all together because, that way, there are fewer variables. By contrast, when you have four musicians playing all at the same time, live, the likelihood for mistakes is duly multiplied by four. Track recording is cleaner and sharper, and it gets quicker results. It is also boring and totally antithetical to jamming, to the essential mess of musical collaboration.

These days, I do a lot less jamming than I used to. But I'm still alive to its influence and, as a listener, I'm always on the hunt for its residue. Call it the scent of the jam, even though it registers as sound: you can catch it now and again on a recording, and it doesn't matter the genre. I'm not talking about live records, which are essentially aural chronicles of formal performances. I'm talking about recordings where there's an element of jam-like enthusiasm or authenticity that spills out and infiltrates the sacred space of the recording. You can hear it, for instance, when Jeff Mangum puts down his guitar at the end of Neutral Milk Hotel's *In the Aeroplane over the Sea*, an album that I once listened to fifty times in a row on the last day that I ever lived in the state of Ohio, in the company of the dozen friends who had come to drink all my booze and help me move. The album does not end cleanly, nor does it fade to acquiescent silence. Instead, there is the pained squeak of the strings as Mangum cuts the final chord. Then comes the hollow knock of his guitar as he sets it down on the floor, then the screech of a chair as he gets up and walks away. On another track on the same album, "Oh Comely," someone in the background—someone there in the room *with* him, somebody watching and listening—yells out: "Holy shit!"

From these minor traces, I can take comfort, as a listener, in knowing that there was once a time, a place, a room, a whole group of people, a jam, and from all of those ingredients came a record of an actual occurrence. It's the actual occurrence that I want, anyway—not something cruelly engineered for consumption, like a veal, inside a box.

These traces of historical occurrence come in many forms. Take, for instance, the pianist Glenn Gould's humming, which settles like gauze over the top of notes programmed by the likes of Bach or Brahms—whatever he happens to be playing on a given recording. Similarly, there are traces to be found in Jeff Buckley's sigh at the beginning of his cover of Leonard Cohen's "Hallelujah" and also in jazz legend Charles Mingus's screams on the opening track of his legendary record *Mingus Ah Um*. These are the moments where the human element of the jam bleeds through the white space of the artifact that was supposed to anesthetize and preserve it. The jam lives, though the container that holds it was already dead from the start.

This is why I can't let Carruth be right, can't let the guy down-stairs win. I say this not simply because I have witnessed the tem-porarily redemptive power of the jam and its effect on the guy downstairs, by which I mean Austin's old neighbor up on the South Side Slopes of Pittsburgh. Rather, I see the longevity of the jam as enduring and inevitable. Unlike the performance, or the record-ing, the jam does not end except for those who turn their backs and stop listening.

Because jamming, like hanging out, asks only one thing of us: it asks for our time. Time is the pure currency that powers the wheels of creative improvisation. Indeed, it is the only thing that can.

4

HANGING OUT ON TV

I once had a friend who was famous and, because she was famous, hanging out with her always meant hanging out twice. We would do it once for ourselves—or if not purely for ourselves, then because we knew that hanging out was socially called for, was necessary. Then we would do it all over again, for the cameras.

Back when my friend first became my friend, it wasn't like this. We first met at a farmers market in Grand Forks, the town in which we both lived at the time. I had recognized her from the internet; she had a successful food blog and, in the months that preceded my relocation to North Dakota, I'd been studying up and trying to figure out what hanging out looked like in the place that was soon to be my home. That led me to her blog, which was dedicated to the juxtaposition of scenes of Midwestern farm life alongside recipes and gossipy anecdotes. Then, one day at the farmers market, I was standing behind her in a checkout line, my arms filled with zucchini. She and I talked, exchanged numbers, and made plans to get together.

And at first, it was all very normal, consisting of dinner parties and the observation of minor holidays, like the Super Bowl. My friend introduced me to hotdish, which is a kind of casserole topped with Tater Tots that is much cherished throughout the upper Midwest. She wasn't from there originally, but hotdish heritage ran deep on her husband's side of the family. The first time I ever lifted a forkful of the stuff to my mouth, I was sitting at my friend's kitchen table, in the house that she shared with her husband, a sugar beet farmer just like his father and his grandfather—the man who built the house we were sitting in—had been. Hanging out with my friend and her husband granted exposure to a kind of crash course in Midwestern culture: not just hotdish but cookie salad, beet harvest "campaigns," bison vs. buffalo, and why Midwesterners never enter anyone's house through the front door, that is, not unless they're selling something.

But then my friend, who was already a little bit famous, became for-real famous with the launch of her very own Food Network reality TV show. For the pilot episode, which was pitched to the network in the hopes of securing a first season's contract, we all played at the work of hanging out, inhabiting hypothetical versions of the people we'd previously tried to be in each other's company. It was exhilarating and also anxious-making; my emotions, I felt, were larger and more pronounced than they might be under normal circumstances. They seemed to take up extra space in the room. The pilot was supposed to be structured around the idea of a Super Bowl party, except we couldn't call it the Super Bowl due to copyright concerns and it was filmed in the fall, months away from the date of the actual game. As participants, we were directed to wear certain colors, act certain ways, and say certain things about the food, which was supposed to have been cooked by my friend but actually wasn't, and which was presented to us and then immediately whisked away, for efficiency's sake, so we could move on to the work of commenting on whatever came right after it.

There were parts of this experience that might have passed for routine. I'd spent two Super Bowls in my friend's living room, ingesting her husband's praise for the Patriots along with hotdish, Scotch eggs (this was a phase for my friend), and deep-fried cheesy pickles. As a result, hanging out in front of television cameras came with a sense of predetermined choreography. I knew what to do because I had done it all before, sort of. But the circumstances were dramatically different this time: there were professional studio lights looming over us, making us sweat, and microphones tucked into our bras. And there were the repeated requests to *Say that thing you just said again, but say it while looking over here, this way.* All of this conspired to rupture the semblance of routine that I had counted on to instill confidence. You never think about how difficult it is to cut a Scotch egg and gracefully ferry a piece of it toward your mouth until you have to do so in front of a bunch of cameras.

My friend's reality TV show became a hit and, in time, the doubleness that came with it started to set in and make itself at home in our lives, to the point where we stopped questioning it, at least out loud. There were two birthdays, two baby showers, two Super Bowls, two hybrid Thanksgiving-Hanukkah parties. One of each, it was assumed, was always supposed to be the real one, which made the other one necessarily less-than-real by default. But we didn't acknowledge this. I was never directly told to pretend to celebrate someone's birthday or to act like it was the Super Bowl when it actually wasn't: words like *pretend* and *act* never bubbled up through the layers of discourse that surrounded these occasions, though they made up a weighty and unavoidable part of the subtext lurking beneath them. Instead, I would receive invitations from the show producers—never from my friend, not anymore—in my email inbox asking if I wanted to be present for a "meal." If I said yes, I would then receive instructions about where to go, what to wear, how to style my hair and makeup, and how much time (sometimes it could be as much as eight hours) to block out of my schedule for the observance of said meal.

Uncanny is the word that comes to mind when I think of what it meant to hang out with my friend on television in this way, but it's not a perfect word. Rather, it's a word that people tend to use when they can't explain something, because the word itself conjures the unexplainable. Sigmund Freud, who popularized the use of the word (or its German language equivalent), actually had something rather specific in mind: "The uncanny is that class of the frightening which leads back to what is known of old and long familiar."[1] It's true that, in hanging out with my friend on TV, in front of a crew of lighting and sound engineers and cameras and producers, I felt like I was returning to something. But it's untrue that the thing itself was something familiar and known to me, something that already existed and could be plucked from a bank of remembered experiences.

For Freud, it's the gap between familiarity and foreignness that breeds monstrousness. Between those two poles exists a chasm of sorts, as Freud sees it, and that's where monstrosity slips in and takes up residence. One can recognize it by its scent, which arises from a confusing mix of the smells of home combined with foreign, slightly feral vapors. This is sort of like the feeling that comes from being recruited to participate in a scene of staged sociality like the kind that happens on reality TV. What is unnerving about the experience is that it brings one into contact with what should be but has never properly been—an idealized vision of friends, life, interconnection, and hanging out. That vision is not exactly "known of old and long familiar," to recall Freud's words, because it is entirely *unknown* to us outside the bounds of TV itself. We are familiar with it as a simulation, yes, but we have never known or experienced it as a literal reality. We have never been there before, though we've seen it mentioned on signs and maps.

The essayist Mark Greif tries to explain this feeling: "There is a persistent dream that television will be more than it is: that it will not only sit in every home, but make a conduit for those homes to reach back to a shared fund of life."[2] That persistent dream *is* the dream of company, of hanging out; it is the dream of living a life that takes place within a safe, self-curated enclosure that nevertheless connects and hooks up to shared, social experience. Greif actually mentions the Food Network and its specific brand of reality shows when he complains of "five hundred channels of identical fluff, network reruns, syndicated programs, second-run movies, infomercials, and home shopping." Thirty years ago, he says, no one could have dreamed of paying for, let alone enjoying, all that identical content.[3] But to see it in this way is to overlook the cyclicality and repetition that reigns over the idea of hanging out itself. Reality television shows—including my friend's—enact these cycles, allowing them to happen again and again and under grander terms than they would normally, injecting freshness into each new instance of ritual. This is why so many viewers feel comforted by them: they know what to expect and, unlike with actual social situations, the results can be counted on. Rarely can our interactions with real, live people yield the luxury of such certitude.

"Our culture is obsessed with real events because we experience hardly any," writes the author and textual collage artist David

Shields.[4] He writes them even though, strictly speaking, these are not his words to write. Rather, he borrows them—Shields is forever borrowing, appropriating, and layering in his work—from two sources: Andrew O'Hehir, writing in *Salon*, and also from the essayist Frank Rich, who Shields thought he was borrowing from until he traced the line back to O'Hehir. The notion expressed in it strikes me as at least half true where reality television is concerned. Like Shields himself, reality television borrows from a generalized understanding of what life is like. That understanding is contained in stories, which is what reality television then tries to manufacture.

Hanging out—real hanging out—is also about stories; in fact, it consists mostly of them. It's a process that sees old stories getting launched into recirculation at the same time that new ones are brought into being. But when you're hanging out on television, for television, the story is already set for you. The element of invention is just a tease, much like the food that kept getting placed in front of me and then taken away again. The result is a kind of impasse, a fixed state of being in which old stories cannot get told and swapped and new ones can't get made. Instead of either, everyone's focus is consumed by a knowledge of the story they're *supposed* to be telling, the one that isn't even true. It's the Super Bowl! (It's October.) It's Hanukkah! (It's April.) It's a baby! (Again—we did this last weekend.)

This is why reality television is often so unsatisfying. We know it is, so we try to fix the problem of our unsatisfaction by consuming more of it. Shields says that this results from two simultaneous conditions of being: as a culture, we are, he claims, both "desperate for authenticity and in love with artifice."[5] In being torn between the two, we ask too much of reality television: we ask it to give us what we want, when what we want involves an unholy synthesis of opposites. This conflict ensures that we go away hungry at the end of each episode, only to return the next time with the same old hopes for nourishment.

There are two conditions for which a feeling of satiation is always temporary for us humans: fellowship and food. Is there any wonder that the most consistent recipe for successful reality television involves both?

The food that we ate together on my friend's reality television show was often delicious. But, like the medium through which our supposed enjoyment of it was broadcast, it was rarely satisfying.

Because viewers who consume reality television cannot personally experience the supposed reality of it—they cannot taste, or smell, or touch that reality—the only thing that really matters is how it looks and how they see it. So the food was always beautiful, and my friend was always beautiful, and we extras were always trying our best to be as beautiful as either her or her food, to match the tenor of the story that had been planned for us. We tried to be beautiful so as not to let everyone down. I tried, at least. Why? Because I wanted to help my friend; because I wanted to be included; because I thought I might make a friend by playing one on TV.

But the ratio between actual hanging out and staged hanging out started to shift. With so much of it happening for the sake of the cameras, we found that there was very little time left over for the real stuff. My interactions with my friend—the ones that happened off-screen—became fewer and fewer. And they also became more diminished somehow, by contrast. Our more humble instances of hanging out, like gathering together in our glum little town's glum

little bowling alley for someone's birthday, started to feel insuffi-
cient in comparison to the elaborate displays that had been scripted
and arranged for us back when it wasn't anyone's birthday.

And then this happened: there came a moment when I realized
that my friend and I probably weren't even friends anymore. What's
ironic is that this moment came about because I had been asked to
furnish proof of our friendship. In anticipation of the baby shower
episode, the producers asked for photos. They wanted to portray
my friend through the ages, in all her many visages, for her viewers. They wanted pictures of us hanging out as teenagers, pictures
of us at parties and holidays—real ones, that is, not the ones we'd
mimed on TV. And I didn't have any of those photos. Or, at least,
I didn't have any that included myself along with my friend (we'd
only known each other for a couple of years, after all), apart from
those that had already been plastered all over the internet back in
her life as a food blogger, or all over the television in her current life
as a name-brand celebrity. The only one I could find was a picture
of my friend and me from a recent Halloween. In it, I was dressed
up as a witch and my friend was dressed up as me.

There is perhaps nothing that comes closer to a mundane and
accessible vision of the uncanny than witnessing someone else's
attempt to impersonate you. Freud talks about this, too, explaining
that, in encountering one's double, or something approximating it, a
person is compelled by an "urge towards defense," the goal of which
is to "project that material out as something foreign" to oneself.[6]
My friend styled her hair in a way I didn't know I styled mine but
then immediately recognized as the way I style mine. She wore a
long, formal coat with a multicolored scarf, channeling some of my
unconscious but still recognizable trademarks. And she carried a

copy of *The House of Mirth* by Edith Wharton, a novel I have written about and also taught many times. My friend knew me—had *read* me, amassing a stockpile of clues about personality and preference, in the way I had used to *read* her back when I was a regular visitor to her blog. And the reading had yielded an image—an essentially correct one, I was terrified to discover, albeit limited to surface detail. Whatever we were to each other, as friends, we had each other's surfaces down.

I gave the photo of my friend and me to her show's producers, even though I knew it wasn't exactly what they were looking for. And, indeed, it didn't make the cut, it wasn't in the made-for-TV slideshow that was used to close the episode. Or, at least, that's what I assumed. I don't know for sure because, to this day, I've never seen an episode of my friend's show. I have avoided it because I don't want to see myself acting like myself: I have tried to waylay the moment of confrontation with my own "double," an event that I know is probably inevitable but also scary as hell. That is one reason. But I also think I've been wanting to preserve some tiny little sliver of the way it used to be for my friend and me, of that thing I had once dared to call friendship. I know that, in watching the pantomime of our friendship on TV, I'll be forced to give that up, whatever it was. And if I do that—if I relinquish the small suggestion of authenticity that, for years, I had been using to chase the bitter flavor of so much artifice—then I'll be left with only the latter and nothing to make it worthwhile or palatable anymore.

Back when we were still very much in each other's lives, I never talked to my friend about not watching her show, but neither did I lie and tell her I had seen it. I often wondered if she could sense the truth and if she did, why she kept inviting me to come along and be a part of it. I kept wondering, in other words, why we kept hanging out after it seemed like there was so little substance to be found at the bottom of our doing that. In the end, I arrived at the realization that she needed me to help her construct a semblance of fun. Television coerces us into believing that fun cannot happen when one is alone, and television is about the ruthless pursuit and presentation of fun. My friend needed people to be her friends on TV, perhaps even more than she needed them to be her friends in real life. She needed those people to distract, in visual terms, from the food, because food is only partly about food—it's mostly about hanging out. The exception comes when the hanging out is bad and then it really is about the food, but only as a last resort.

When I left North Dakota in the summer of 2020, my friend and I hadn't seen in each other in months and we didn't say goodbye. I can't even be sure when she realized that I wasn't there anymore. Was it when I failed to respond to a show producer's invitation to yet another "meal"?

   In my new home in Vermont, I joined a gym that insisted, for some reason, on blasting the Food Network from one of its dozens of mounted flat-screen TVs. I was rowing one day on the rowing machine when I looked up and straight into the face of my friend. A new season of the show was being advertised and, in the background, I could see quick slices of my old life flashing past. I saw the farm and the fields of already-harvested beets with their rows frozen solid and crusted with wintry detritus. I saw my friend's kitchen and her pistachio-colored refrigerator; I remembered how, once, I'd been directed to dress in complementary tones. I saw the table where I'd had my first taste of hotdish.

I saw the other people who had participated and hung out on the show when I had hung out on the show—people who must have been my friends, too, once, because didn't they used to invite me to hang out sometimes, and didn't I still have their numbers stored in my cell phone?

According to Greif, standardized programming—including reality TV, which is the only content that is cheap enough to make the proliferation of five-hundred-plus channels economically possible in the first place—tends to erase regional differences:

> Reality television may furnish its [nationalized media's] dark apotheosis—a form for an era in which local TV has been consolidated out of existence, regional differences are said to be diminishing (or anyway less frequently represented), and news, increasingly at the service of sales departments, has forfeited its authority to represent the polity.[7]

My friend's show was supposed to revolve around the authentic presentation of regional difference. Thus, on the surface, it sometimes looked and felt like it was out to prove Greif wrong. But it played at a kind of clumsy portraiture, representing Midwestern culture with brushstrokes that were so thick and broad, they obscured the fact that the show's participants (myself included) mostly hailed from outside the region. The idea was to present the grandeur and charm of regional difference without focusing too much on the details that might show the chinks in that vision of reality. And at the heart of that reality lies an assumption about how hanging out is supposed to work. It's supposed to be the same everywhere, we are told, though the costumes and scenery may differ.

Reality television conjures situations that look and feel familiar—that feel canny, in other words, if we take this word to mean what it meant in sixteenth-century Scots English. *Canny* comes from the Scots word *can*, which later became *ken*, meaning "to know." Freud had a similar, though slightly different, definition in mind when he developed his arguments surrounding what he called, in German, the *unheimlich*, the literal translation of which amounts to an "un-home-like" feeling. Thus, something that is canny, or something *heimlich*, is something that is knowable and reminiscent of home, while something that is uncanny, or *unheimlich*, forces us to confront the fact of our not understanding. It names the point at which we stop, look around, and suddenly discover ourselves to be very far from home. This point opens onto that previously mentioned chasm, into which our confidence in lived experience begins to roughly slide, to our great horror and confusion. But it is framed on either side by a landscape that feels disconcertingly familiar. This is reality television's plot: it masks an essential uncanniness through its repeated attempts to make everything feel homely and essentially tame. Then, because what is tame is also somewhat boring, it splashes a few local details haphazardly about. What results is comparable to a child's drawing. The shapes are recognizable to us—dog, tree, house—but they are also alien, smothered under a lurid weight of color.

I, being a transplant to the Midwest, was not immune to fantasies of authenticity and inclusion. In fact, I was swept up by them, sold on the promise of authenticity that is the business of television, itself a prime instrument of artifice. I thought that by claiming a position for myself within the authentic pageantry of the Midwest, I might learn how to become a part of it. So I went along with it, donning the costumes as necessary, which, for the baby shower episode, meant "light spring florals," though we filmed in February inside my friend's unheated barn. I remember kneeling on the freezing concrete floor, shivering in my spring florals as the crew pumped lightly vaporized air into the space of the barn so that our breaths wouldn't show on TV.

One of the writers who has been most central to my thinking about hanging out and, in particular, about doing so in the Midwest is Meridel Le Sueur. Le Sueur was born in 1900, at the very beginning of "the most brutal century, the twentieth century," as she puts it in a documentary film made toward the end of her life, in 1976.[8] Her parents were proud leftists and did not seek to shield her from an awareness of the world's brutality. Her stepfather, Arthur Le Sueur, was the first and only socialist mayor of Minot, North Dakota, and was an early member of that state's leading progressive political faction, the Nonpartisan League; her mother, Marian Le Sueur, taught English at the radical People's College located in Fort Scott, Kansas, until it was burned by anti-socialist vigilantes in 1917.[9] The family fled north following that event, settling in St. Paul, Minnesota, which was to be the launching point for Le Sueur's own activities as a writer. Her best-known work, the 1939 novel *The Girl*, takes place there, in Minnesota, but it wasn't published until 1978 due to Le Sueur's having been blacklisted and banned from print beginning in the 1940s.

A friend of mine sent me a link to that documentary about Le Sueur during what was, for me, a very difficult time. I had just decided to leave the Midwest, a place that was not my original home but had finally just started to feel like a viable replacement for all the homes I had lost over the years. The documentary, called

My People Are My Home, was produced by the Twin Cities Women's Film Collective. It consists of nothing but Le Sueur's voice and words, layered over images of Midwestern life—the landscape, yes, but also church socials, dances, suppers, harvest parties, parades, picket lines, union halls, classrooms, and assemblies. It's one of the truest and most comforting documents of Midwestern life I've ever encountered. In it, Le Sueur's voice sounds commandingly resonant but singed at the edges, burned out from use and from age. With this rich, slightly battered voice of hers, she begins the film by addressing the prairie directly, saying, "I can never leave you. I have stayed with you, being in love with you, bent upon understanding you, bringing you life. For your life is my life and your death is mine also."[10] The film, like all of Le Sueur's work, is a love letter to both a place and a people, both of them endangered by the time of its creation, both of them scarred from too much life lived on the brink of a limitless and lonely peril.

I am not sure that I ever managed to authentically experience even half of what Le Sueur describes in her writings about the Midwest, though I can't say I didn't try. My efforts led me to become a part of my friend's show, though that choice, ironically enough, probably served to engineer the opposite result. What never came through on the show were all the parts of Midwestern life that weren't pretty enough for TV but actually made life in the region enjoyable. These are, significantly, also the parts that would be right at home in the Le Sueur documentary. These places and people continue to live in my memory, but not through coordinated neutrals and spring florals. Rather, they occupy a part of my brain that is saturated with the warm, orangey tints of a 1970s Kodachrome Super 8 film montage. This is the way my friend's living room appears to me now, in retrospect, with its wood veneer paneling and television nestled amongst a scaffolding of bowed, homemade bookshelves. Likewise the machine shop on the farm—that's where we celebrated the end of the beet harvest each year with hot dogs and plates of store-bought macaroni salad and maybe, now and then, hotdish. These scenes form the antithesis of the made-for-TV aesthetic. They can't be broadcast to the world; they would melt and liquefy under the glare of all that professional-grade lighting.

The people who I met and gathered alongside in these spaces, who filled them up, were, likewise, my home. They arrived dressed three-layers deep in wool and down if it was winter, and then took ten minutes to remove all the layers and pile them on the overloaded coat hooks in the hall. They left a heap of boots and shoes by the door and then approached on stocking feet to ask about a good place to put the seven-layer salad they'd brought along. If I could make a film about them, I'd channel Le Sueur's voice to tell a story about the time my friend secretly slipped a piece of cake into the pocket of my big down overcoat, which was hanging in the hall with the others, because she knew that, on my walk home, I'd put my hands into my pockets and be excited to discover cake. (I did; I was.)

My friend made a career for herself out of making and proffering cake, but also out of having and being friends with people on TV. I helped her do it, at least for a while. It was a way of making the little place that we inhabited a bit larger, I think—a means of pushing against its boundaries to see if we could open it up and let some more of the world in. Le Sueur reminds us that all of us, but Midwesterners in particular, "emerge from the little place." And it's after we emerge from it that we start to look back over our shoulders to see if the people we remember from that little place are still standing behind us. And it's after we see that they aren't that we come to finally know what it meant for them to have stood there once before.

This is the hole in contemporary social life that cannot be made better or healed by TV, but it is also what we continually ask TV—especially reality TV—to do for us. We come to TV on our hands and knees and we ask it to make it better, to stitch it back together, to give us all the places, including both the ones we had and the ones we never will. We beg TV to beam those places and people into the enclosures where we live now so we can have someone to talk to and hang out with.

HANGING OUT

ON THE

5

JOB

There was a wedding happening in the hotel too.

The guests had spilled out onto the balconies that overlooked the hotel bar, dangling the sherbet shades of their evening wear over the railings, clutching at champagne glasses and tiny beaded purses. In the first-floor ladies' room, they congregated before the mirrors to hitch things up or pull things down, to conduct between-stall conversations of a highly personal nature, and to reapply lipstick and splash their pastel business all around.

I was jealous. I envied their giggles and their out-loudness and also the creamy sweep of their skirts as they moved over the lobby's tiled floors. I was dressed in the sober tones of business-casual banality and feeling self-consciously black and blue. But in the moments when I came close to them, the wedding guests, I could feel their colors catching, transmitting a feverish warmth up through my arms and legs. It was a study in cruel contrasts: up on the balconies, all rainbows and sequins and champagne and bass rhythms; down below, at the bar, the black-clad backs of the academic-conference crowd, low-voiced snark, watered-down scotch.

I was standing a few paces away from the bar, tucked into protective shadow, and feeling just drunk enough to remember to be afraid of everyone around me.

I had felt like that—exposed, on display—for the entirety of the conference. It was because of what had happened the first night, with Henry, whose name, rest assured, is not really Henry. It was a thing that I could not undo or void or amend, a thing that had since clung to the surface of my brain like a diseased growth. It was a thing I hadn't seen coming—that most exciting species of thing, a *misunderstanding*. Henry had wanted something from me that I hadn't wanted to give and then, later on, he had decided he didn't want it anymore, had never wanted it, would never dream of wanting it from someone like me. He had made a point of telling this to me and, I suspected, many others at the conference as well. The *misunderstanding* was, in truth, not a misunderstanding at all, but I sensed this word was his way of waving the whole thing away.

I should have seen it coming, was all I could think. Why wasn't I smart enough to see it coming? At my weaker moments, I chalked it up to professional naivete, combined with maybe a constitutional inability to say no. These thoughts wrestled with my desire to resist the easy and orthodox logic of feminine weakness. Because, I kept reminding myself, a person doesn't need to see something coming in order to say no to it.

I was locked away inside myself and thinking about all of this when, upstairs at the wedding, Junior Walker and the All Stars started playing. A trampling of feet along the carpeted corridor, squealed indications of approval: the DJ knew his crowd. Downstairs, I continued to hang at the margins of the bar, waiting for the brandy to stop burning its way through my belly.

There had been a group dinner reservation but then Henry had disinvited me, because of the *misunderstanding*. Not in person, of course. He hadn't spoken to me since that first night. But he had sent me a text message. *I'm sure you'll agree that it's probably better if* . . . And he'd made dramatic efforts to avoid me, always exiting a room whenever I walked into it. Which is how I had found myself without dinner plans that night and at the behest of serendipity. Not by myself, thankfully: I had the company of an old friend, a former faculty mentor of mine who was also attending the conference. Together, he and I had left the hotel in search of things that were not the hotel or its assorted occupants. We had roamed the streets of a city I already hoped to never return to—a city I was only in because Henry had insisted that I be there, insisted I join the panel he had organized but that I somehow ended up organizing.

We had stopped walking, this mentor-friend and I, when we encountered what had looked like a dark, sparsely occupied bar that turned out to be a dark, sparsely occupied Iranian restaurant. It was the kind of place where the owner worked the bar while his wife and sisters worked the kitchen and his children and nieces and nephews kept the dining room covered, delivering baskets of still-warm pita to the tables alongside saucers of olive oil. We hadn't known what to do when the glasses of Courvoisier started showing up, unbidden. Turned out, it was the restaurant's grand opening; the owner, smiling at us over the bar, wouldn't take no for an answer.

Afterward, my mentor-friend had headed off to bed at the hotel; he had an early flight to catch. And I had kept walking. I was trying to rid myself of it, meaning the whole great *misunderstanding*, trying to wriggle free of its weight. But it was there, sometimes lashed to my back and sometimes dragging along behind me, always insistent. Which is why, when I got back to the hotel again, I found I couldn't get into the elevator.

They were the clear glass kind of elevators, you see—positioned at either end of the main lobby and designed so that everyone there could keep tabs on everyone else at such events as ours. They zipped up and down inside their clear glass chambers and bequeathed a bird's-eye view of the lobby to their occupants, and the inverse of that to those gathered below in the center of the panoptic hell that was the hotel bar, where the sherbet crowd now mingled with the black-and-blues. I couldn't deal with being seen in that way, not while I still held all the complimentary Courvoisier on the inside and wore the thing, the *misunderstanding*, all over me on the outside.

I opted for the stairs instead. I found them just beyond a sign marked PRIVATE EVENT.

When I got to the second floor, though, I was ambushed by color: rich purples and reds, shimmering riffs on orange and peach, neons, slippery approximations of silver and gold that refused to sit still in my eyes. And the accessories, the hats and the gloves and the tiny purses and the trailing skirts and the *scarves*, long, diaphanous waves that followed in the wake of the wearer, writing color on the air. Someone pressed a glass of something into my hand.

It wasn't that I couldn't say no to Henry, whose name, once again, is not Henry. Rather, I felt bound to a masochistic desire to win the approval of those who seemed least likely to ever give it to me. I wanted to say no without having to say it, so as to keep the possibility of approval on the table. It was a perverse form of want, a kind of Stockholm syndrome of the soul, and it had been the basis of much of my professional training up to this point. I had spent so many years learning to want that which I did not need in order to succeed or be good in the ways I wanted to be. How to go about unlearning it.

I was thinking these things, digesting them along with the brandy, as I melted into the crowd there on the dance floor. I stayed for a few hours and then was among the last to leave it. By the time I did, returning to the elevators, my body glowing with exhaustion, I had forgotten my former fears about being seen.

Which was good because Henry was there inside the elevator. Not alone, of course. He was with another woman my age, no doubt working on his next *misunderstanding*. He said something, pointed to the turquoise scarf that was draped about my neck and to the open bottle of red wine that was poking out of my laptop bag. I had worn a laptop bag to a wedding. Well, it was okay, it was a wedding I hadn't meant to attend, one that gave out half-empty bottles of red wine and colored scarves as favors, apparently. I laughed, loudly, when I got done processing all of this.

Henry was fifteen years older than me, with tangles of gray hair mounded atop his brow and a wife and kids back home. He was famous for his *misunderstandings* with women like me; I didn't know it then, but there in the elevator with him and his next candidate, I was starting to know it. He had made a career out of such *mis-understandings*. In a few more years, I would witness his expulsion from a conference just like this one on account of them. But there in the elevator, I saw him trying for innocence and smiles. He was doing his best to look fragile, and he did, in a way, like a plate glass window begging for a brick.

That night, I lacked the strength to be the one to throw it. But since then, I've grown stronger. I've inserted myself into a variety of professional conference scenes, made friends, met new colleagues, traveled places. I still see him, in lots of them.

The story I have been telling here is many stories. It's the story of the time I attended the opening of an Iranian restaurant, for instance. It's the story of how I accidentally crashed a stranger's wedding that was taking place in the same hotel as a conference I was attending. And it's the story of how I learned to hang out at conferences, which is also the story of how I, through substantial suffering, learned how *not to* hang out conferences. That last story, by the way, is a common one. Many members of my profession, especially female members, likely already know it by heart.

My version of that story lacks a clearly identified villain because, even now, years later, I fear the professional consequences that might arise from stating his name. So it's a vague story and fated, for a variety of reasons, to remain that way. But it's also a launching point: the conference I have been describing was the beginning of my involvement in a regular conference scene. Since then, my yearly professional calendar has been organized by conferences in a way that compares to how those of nineteenth-century New York *Social Register*—style elites were organized by parties and balls. Or, at least, my calendar used to be organized in this way. Now that situation is in flux, thanks not just to the lingering effects of the COVID pandemic but, likewise, ongoing changes to the structure of academia.

For scholars like myself, conferences serve the primary function of expanding the sphere of one's professional activities. In my line of scholarship, for example, which involves the teaching of English literature and writing, conferences provide opportunities for extended education. At them, participants give public presentations based on their research and receive feedback—sometimes immediately, in the form of live questions from the audience, and sometimes in a delayed sense through conversations that might take place hours, days, or months afterward, through remote means like email or, even, publication. Conferences thus exist to foster conditions of reciprocity: in addition to speaking and presenting, an attendee also listens and witnesses talks given by others in her field. All of this activity occurs under an umbrella of intellectual cross-pollination. The seeds of that activity get scattered upon the wind once the event concludes and participants return home to their respective campuses, which are duly nourished as a result.

That, at least, is what we say. It's what we have to say in order to gain funding from our home institutions to attend these conferences (in certain fields, like the hard sciences, funding can be quite generous, but within the arts and humanities sectors, it is on the decline, to the point where many professionals in those disciplines now pay their own ways). But, as ever, the shadow agenda of hanging out is there. While it purports to serve, and often succeeds in serving, other, seemingly more legitimate purposes, a conference is also fundamentally about seizing the opportunity to hang out. This is the illegitimate side of conference-going and, for many people, it's also the main one. Mind you, I use the word *illegitimate* in this instance not because I believe there is no value to be found in this style of hanging out, but because I know that others see it this way. Nobody wants to pay someone to hang out, even if that hanging out happens on the weekend (as all conferences in my field do) and thus serves to prolong the hours of the regular working week, the *legitimate* working week. Fun, after all, is supposed to be anathema to work, which is why the prospect of fun gets treated like a contagion. Fun threatens to infect and pervert the sanctity of labor and also the power of those who would have us do more of it, for free, by cramming more into the slim, preexisting spaces of paychecks and contracts. Fun, so this brand of managerial thinking goes, is an illegitimate use of company time since it doesn't produce anything or make anybody richer.

It is this view, I think, that inspires the maniacal interest in fun, revelry, and hanging out that I have witnessed at professional conferences. That and, for many in my field, conferences are also reunions—with old graduate school colleagues, with old students, with old coworkers from previous universities and academic posts (modern academics are forced to move around a lot), and with the kind of intellectual comrades who might work in our respective fields but very rarely in the same buildings, cities, or even states as us. Academic work rests on the twin pursuits of writing and research, activities that demand fair degrees of isolation. Conferences furnish productive disturbances to, or breaks from, that isolation. They appear to us like little islands, calling to us when we've been adrift for many months at sea. That is why we attend them; that is why many of us, even, will pay for the privilege of doing so. They are like conceptual jam sessions—charmed locales that play host to experimentation, improvisation, and the fruitful clash of ideas. What gets created from that clash can be nothing, or it can be something that requires months or years of further gestation. But it can also be something suddenly solid and real: a new venture, a new research question, a new source to consult, a new collaboration.

The last big, in-person conference I attended was the Modern Language Association (MLA) Convention, held in Seattle in January 2020, which at the time was hailed jointly as both the beginning of a new era and the end of an old one. That MLA conference saw the lowest attendance in over forty years, and that was before COVID came along to further deplete the event's numbers. But it also marked the beginning of a new organizational outlook: the MLA had begun to officially sanction the use of remote technologies to conduct job interviews. For decades, those interviews had been occurring in person at the convention itself, often in hotel suites that were rented by interview committees representing various schools. The MLA organization, though, had finally come around not only to the existence of technologies that rendered such inter views unnecessary, but likewise to the financial burdens that the old system placed on interviewees. Not all schools, you see, pay for their faculty members to attend conferences, and even fewer of them pay for their graduate students to do so, though it is graduate students who are usually there to interview for jobs.

The shift to remote interviews is one reason that attendance at MLA, and other academic conferences like it, has been on the decline. But it's not the only reason. The bigger reason is that there are fewer jobs to interview for in the first place, now that the vast majority of faculty positions in higher education have been casualized—reduced, that is, to highly exploitative, part-time versions of their formerly tenured selves. The numbers vary by types of institutions and degrees, but sources like the American Association of University Professors report that anywhere between 60 and 80 percent of instruction at undergraduate degree–granting colleges and universities in the United States is done by this other, part-time population.[1] These professors are often called adjuncts, or else by titles that offer creative glosses on the term *adjunct* (as in Senior Lecturer, Visiting Associate Professor, Teaching Professor, etc.), and, along with being denied

benefits and fair pay, they do not often receive funding to attend conferences. This means that they don't go to conferences, usually. This
means that conferences—at least as professors used to conceive of
them—are dying, and that less hanging out and cross-pollination is
happening now as a result.

This is a problem because hanging out is networking and networking is, as the term itself suggests via its inclusion of the original
word, *work*. It was there, for instance, at what I have been calling
the worst conference of my life, that my own career as a writer
started to take off. I had been disinvited from all of the things I had
been previously invited to, by a man who was exacting his revenge
for my apparent failure to understand his true intentions. A *misunderstanding*, he called it, which it was not: it was an imposition, an
incursion of the oldest and most cliché kind. But his hybrid shame-
vengeance helped to free up my conference dance card, so to speak,
and resulted in new opportunities for improvisation. I was free to
roam and to fashion new associations. I didn't know anyone at the
conference, aside from the man in question and my old faculty mentor, who had dipped in only momentarily, for the space of a single
evening. Everything else and everyone else was new to me. So I
hung out. (Okay, I spent an entire night crying in my hotel room
first; *then* I hung out.)

I attended panels and asked questions of the speakers. I concocted lunch plans with strangers. I accepted a last-minute, emergency spot as a panel moderator, because the original one had
backed out, and introduced speakers who were presenting on topics
I knew nothing about. I learned things. I made small talk at happy
hours. And yes, I got drunk on free Courvoisier and accidentally
crashed a stranger's wedding. But I also left the conference with

arrangements in place for a new publication, with cell phone numbers and contacts, and with a stranger's credit card, even (okay, that
part was a mistake—the restaurant's, not mine). That is to say, I left
that conference with the beginnings of a collegial network that has
continued to support and sustain me.

The worst conference I ever attended turned out to be the best
conference I ever attended. And all because disaster, and the whims
of a "known predator," as I later heard someone at another conference describe him, had forced me to make it that way for myself.

~~~~~

There's a scene in Tom McCarthy's novel *Satin Island* in which the
protagonist, a "corporate anthropologist" known only as U., fanta-
sizes about an ideal conference experience. He begins by renovating
the space of the conference venue itself, turning it into something
more dignified and grandiose:

> In my mind's eye, the hi-tech modern conference hall
> morphed into a nineteenth- or even eighteenth-century
> auditorium: steep-banked rows of wooden benches, an
> audience made up exclusively of men with bushy sideburns
> and high collars, pipe- and cigar-smoke mingling with mur-
> murs of approval in air already thick with erudition and just
> plain old age—although I still had a projector wi-fi'd to a
> sensor on my index finger, split-second responsive.[2]

U. has a deep desire to be hailed as a conference hero. This is
because his experience has yielded the opposite: he has recently

given a presentation that was "met with silence, then, when my audience realized that I'd finished, a smattering of polite clapping. No one approached me to discuss it afterwards."[3] In fact, when he meets a fellow conference attendee later on that evening, in the hotel sauna, he is denied recognition and, even, eye contact. His colleague pretends not to notice him.

Sensing his designation, then, as a real-life persona non grata, U. dreams of becoming the inverse, of seeing his colleagues hail him as the conference's indisputable star. He conjures visions in which, rather than being met with silence, his presentation results in "cheering so clamorous" that he is "forced to come back time and again, to take another bow." U. imagines "delegates . . . surging forwards, address books open, business cards stretched out towards me, their numbers overwhelming the security personnel who tried to hold them back."[4] His vision is a compensatory one, of course, meant to alleviate the humiliation he has been forced to suffer in reality. But it's also, I think, a relatable kind of fantasy, one that taps into the secret desires of many a professional conference-goer.

Despite what I've been saying about them with regard to rowdiness and hanging out, professional conferences tend to be pretty decorous, straight-laced events. Often, a speaker's presentation is, just as McCarthy describes, met with silence, followed maybe by a trickle of polite applause. Often, though, it is much worse than that: there is nobody there to hear it in the first place, and the panel participants present only to each other. I count myself lucky to have been spared the embarrassment of delivering a conference paper to no one, or to a mere audience of other panelists. But I've heard about it happening, have come close to having it happen, and have nearly witnessed it happening to others. Once, at a conference, while I was enjoying some complimentary coffee in the hotel lobby, an organizer rushed in to tell me that a panel was beginning that featured all graduate students. Could I please attend, she begged, and maybe grab a few others and wrangle them into coming with me? I did exactly that, grabbing a couple of nearby conference-goers and explaining the situation. Together, we made up a supportive little audience of four, which was just enough to outweigh the three terrified panel participants, who looked to be first-time presenters.

McCarthy, though, channels a very sympathetic set of fears when he has protagonist in *Satin Island* indulge in wistful dreams of what could have been. For a conference is always an exercise in fantasy, an exercise in subjecting oneself to the caprices of what could be, when what could be *can*, in fact, be disastrous. McCarthy's U. is nervous and high-strung, at points convinced by his own genius and the value of his "racket," as he deprecatingly labels his work in corporate anthropology,[5] and at other points cognizant of his status as "prey"—yet another intellectual driven by the craving for a kind of "purity" that is "no more than a state in which all frames of comprehension, of interpretation and analysis, are lacking." U. tries to explain this situation to a drunk woman he meets in a bar, observing that once these deficient frames of understanding or comprehension are "brought to bear, the mystery that drew the anthropologist towards his subject in the first place vanishes."[6] His point is that ignorance is, indeed, bliss and its opposite, knowledge, generally entails an ill-fated search for something that cannot be apprehended.

I have seen such devastation on display at conferences, which can also serve as venues for group catharsis where academic and creative work are concerned. But I have also seen plenty of the reverse, including solidarity, support, encouragement, and collaboration. Once, at a conference, I saw a very prominent scholar—someone who is known for performing, with great intensity and enthusiasm, his disagreement with almost anything he hears in such arenas— give a thorough dressing-down to a graduate student presenter, to the point of bringing her to tears. It was an ugly scene, yet it inspired an immediate groundswell of support from the audience, who stepped in to defend her arguments and insights, to temper the prominent scholar's comments, and to compliment her work and her bravery. After it was over, I saw a cluster of people gathered around her in the hallway, congratulating her, while the prominent scholar went slinking off alone.

Conferences are a primary way in which people who do jobs like mine seek to hang out on the job. Sometimes, that means dragging one's complaints and hang-ups about the job that they happen to do into the space of public exposure and debate. Sometimes, it means dragging other hang-ups—intimate ones, personal ones, born from insecurities about the quality and meaning of the work that one does—into that same space and then seeking to compensate for them through predatory acts. But then there are those times when the hanging out proves to be productive and emancipatory. It can free a person from the more stultifying and familiar confines of what normally qualifies as work for them, and it can remind them why they do that work in the first place.

For instance, back when I lived in North Dakota, in a place that felt as intellectually remote as it did geographically, conferences became very important to my progress as a thinker. They provided places where I could go to test and try new ideas, or else to learn about ideas I hadn't yet started to think about. And, just as I found myself living far away from friends and colleagues, and stumbling through the motions of making new ones, conferences gave me a social context that I could count on, a place I could keep returning to. They gave me back my old friends and support systems, at least temporarily, and also bestowed new ones. They gave me a place to work that was not the place that I *had* to work, and they allowed me to keep a foothold in a world that had started to feel very foreign.

I learned about what it means to hang out on the job from attending professional conferences. But even before that, I gained exposure to introductory lessons on the subject from being a bartender. Working a job like that in fact means working two: there are the required physical duties, like dispensing beer (glass held at an angle, not too much head), doing dishes (no dishwasher means *dunk, dunk, dunk*— soap, rinse, bleach), wiping down the bar, and taking the money; then there are the other duties, the shadow agenda of every service worker, which largely amount to hanging out.

I started working as a bartender when I was twenty-three years old. This was in Washington state, at a little bar located in a sparsely settled corner of its Olympic Peninsula. The place where I worked was to be found at the terminus of a dead-end road, adjacent to an entrance to the peninsula's only real attraction, Olympic National Park. It was the sole establishment of its kind for miles—about thirty miles to be precise, since that was the distance to the nearest town, Clallam Bay. Our location there, at a place that maps insisted on calling Ozette (though there was no town there to complement the name), was so remote that we couldn't get kegs delivered. Instead, once a week, my boss, Rob, and I would pile into an old van that he had modified for the purpose of fetching his own, meaning its insides had been stripped of all but the driver's seat. We would pick up the kegs in Clallam Bay and exchange them for empties, completing the sixty-mile circuit that was necessary to keep the bar running and the customers coming. Sometimes, if there was only one to pick up, I'd make the trip alone and strap the lone keg into the front seat of my Honda Civic.

All of this is to say: we were in a lonely place, a far-flung place, a sodden little hermitage of gray and green. Washington's Olympic Peninsula is famous for its rain, which falls with unrelenting grace, and with few interruptions in the form of temperature fluctuations, throughout the majority of the year. Clallam Bay receives an annual average of 100 inches of rain, which is more than three times that of Seattle, the city where I was born and raised. When I moved out to the peninsula to take a job at Rob's bar, I knew it would be rainy, but I hadn't fully anticipated the isolating effects of all that rain, how it kept folks locked inside and separate, how it drove their desperate search for conviviality and sent them groping for even the most paltry forms of companionship. Our bar was where many of them came to find it, which is how I learned that the job I had been hired to perform—the real job, you might say—was that of providing company.

I came to like this job and also to discover that I was good at it. I liked getting to know the customers. There were two main groups of them and each had its own conversational beat: the locals mostly complained, talking politics and the government, gas prices, land use regulations, and the slow death of the logging industry, to which many of them were still attached; the tourists, meanwhile, tended to ask questions, wanting to know about bear and mountain lion sightings, the weather, tide tables, distances between points, the location of rumored petroglyphs, and other local knowledge. Rob, who had long since grown tired of those questions, maintained a mental inventory of stock responses. To the question, *What kind of fish are in the lake?* he would always reply, *The kind that breathe water.* I, however, was fresh and new and thus still happy to salute tourists' curiosities. This was, I realized, another important part of my job. I had been hired to deflect unwanted small talk, to shield Rob from it and thus save him from the work of feigning cheer for every stranger who came through the door.

I worked five days a week at the bar, but it was on my days off that I was really forced to confront the social limits of my surroundings. I was living on Rob's property, in a rented, single-wide trailer that sat parked directly behind the bar. When the sun was shining, which it almost never was, I would devote my days off to hiking, canoeing, or swimming in the lake—anything to escape the trailer's permanent aroma of rot. But when it was raining, I had nowhere to go that didn't involve driving those sixty miles round trip to the little library in Clallam Bay, which was about the only place where a person could loiter without being called out for doing so. The thought of having to fill my car's gas tank, though, usually prevented me from going there. Instead, I'd spend rainy days holed up in my trailer reading book after book—chain-reading, I called it—until the silence became too unnerving. Then I would relocate to the bar, to the place where I spent all the days that I didn't have off. I'd fold myself into a corner of it and play at invisibility while still reaping the benefits of social proximity, lulled by the low murmur of locals' complaints. Seeing me there, though, Rob would often forget that he had given me the day off and would try to put me to work, despite my attempts to ignore or evade him.

It was those rainy days off that showed me how the land-scape, the weather, and the scattered civic infrastructure of the place had conspired to make even mundane social interactions difficult. It made me sympathize, too, with those who came to the bar every night, less because they wanted to drink, many of them, than because they wanted to gather somewhere that was not home. They would settle in booths or on barstools, looking to warm their hands at the meager fire of what little community might be found at Rob's because, like me, they had nowhere else to go. I got to know them all: the loggers and ex-loggers, the rangers and park staff from down the road, the tourists who had fled their waterlogged campsites, the local UPS delivery driver who might have covered as many as 150 miles that day on his route, the aspir-ing organic farmers, and the tribal members who came from the nearby reservation, which was designated as dry. They all came and they all drank, or else they didn't, or else they tried not to drink and then they ended up doing it anyway. Inside the bar, the options were few but there *were* options, including people, satellite TV, a piano, and a jukebox; outside of it, meanwhile, were all the familiar menaces—long evenings, ruthless rain, and a deep, almost unbreakable country quiet.

They came to see me, too, and that was also the truth of it—the one I had to face up to. For the locals, it was because I was from the "outside," and that meant I was something of a spectacle, a face they weren't already used to seeing every day. For the others, it was because I was a link to the world they had left behind in traveling to Ozette; for them, I was an ambassador from that remembered land and, perhaps, a little more experienced when it came to navi-gating the seemingly alien, hostile territory of the peninsula. Both populations claimed me and did their best to claim my attention as well. So complete were those claims that, come the end of a long shift, I would register a bodily complaint, a deep hunger for peace and silence and inconspicuousness. That feeling would send me into hiding in my trailer for a period of eight to twelve hours, and then the whole process would start over again.

These were the two inescapable extremes of my life there: total exposure and availability at work, or total seclusion and silence when not at work.

~~~~~~

What I longed for, back then at Ozette, were places in between, those "providing the means for people to gather easily, inexpensively, regularly, and pleasurably."[7] The sociologist Ray Oldenburg calls them "third places" in his in 1991 book *The Great Good Place*, and also in other, subsequent works. Third places, as he explains, are not homes ("first places") and they are not places of work ("second places"); they exist apart from the structures of both domesticity and professionalism; they are accessible, affordable, lively, and, above all, public arenas in which people are permitted to congregate without deferring to stated terms of inclusion or exclusion. They take the form of coffee shops, libraries, cafés, bars, general stores, parks, and squares—spaces which might, at first glance, appear to have little in common apart from their publicness. But these places are, Oldenburg argues, a necessary requirement for the prevention of social malaise. Without them, the members of a given society are consigned to patterns of movement that take them from their homes (places that are organized by the logic of ownership, property, and exclusion) to work (places that conform to industrial hierarchies and so are characterized by evaluation and the constant measuring of one's worth) and back again.

Such restricted movement between work and home is a problem, Oldenburg claims, because "social well-being and psychological health depend upon community. It is no coincidence that the 'helping professions' became a major industry in the United States as suburban planning helped destroy local public life and the community support it once lent."[8] What Oldenburg is saying is that where communal life and social infrastructure are lacking, individuals find themselves forced to *pay* for access to support systems. This means that, rather than talking to a family member, we book an appointment with a therapist; rather than asking a neighbor if we can borrow a tool or get help with a physical task, we purchase equipment or someone else's labor and have them do it; rather than exercising with a friend, we pay a personal trainer to motivate and steer us toward our fitness goals.

It is not my intention here, nor is it Oldenburg's, to discount the way that expertise comes into play in all of these scenarios. For instance, a trained therapist will have access to information, insight, and resources that a sympathetic friend or family member might not, just as a chef has the skills to produce a more sophisticated meal than many a home cook. But the point is that such expertise is, all too often, beside the point, or else not necessary for the accomplishment of what are actually basic social objectives. A person who is seeking company is not the same as a person who requires the help of a therapist, but in lieu of other options, paying for therapy might just be that first person's only choice. What's more, when we pay people to perform those traditionally communal functions, life can get pretty expensive.

The same is true of space: what we can't agree to share has to be bought and paid for on an individual basis. As Oldenburg explains, "In the absence of informal public life and informal public spaces, living becomes more expensive. Where the means and facilities for relaxation and leisure are not publicly shared, they become the objects of private ownership and consumption."[9] In other words, if you don't have a local park that your children can walk to, you wind up building a playset in your own backyard, one that you pay for yourself; there, your children can play, but they can't gain exposure to the kinds of social challenges that are the unique provenance of interactions between strangers. Meanwhile, your neighbors are also building their own playsets in their own backyards. A neighborhood becomes an archipelago of backyard playsets, each one frequented, though not consistently, by children with shared household affiliations. Like plays with like. At the same time, the need for yard space—or, if you live in a harsh climate, for indoor space as well—is suddenly greater. The average house size starts to metastasize; the market for housing grows more expensive, squeezing out low-wage earners, who can't afford their own backyards and playsets and so send their children out into the streets to play, in neighborhoods that are increasingly deemed "bad" or "dangerous" by those with private backyard playgrounds. The rhetoric of "bad" and "dangerous" provides a ready-made excuse for keeping these populations, and their offspring, apart from each other, and the material divide between them continues to expand.

Third places exist to span the divide between rich and poor, between the backyard playset class and the playing-in-the-street class, and to make the experience of being around different kinds of people feel habitual, meaning both more likely and less threatening.

One of the things I appreciated about Rob's bar was its ability to do this, albeit on a pretty humble scale. The bar tried its best to be many things to many people—too many, some might say (it still exists and, when I'm feeling particularly masochistic, I sometimes resort to skimming Google reviews of the place, which never fail to serve up a welter of class-based accusations and complaints from tourists). It tried, in other words, to be a third place in a region where no others like it existed, to mediate between the various populations that gravitated seasonally to Ozette while still finding a way to serve the locals, who were more or less confined to the area. But this often proved exhausting for Rob, who lived upstairs above the bar, just steps away from his own place of work. The community's only functional third place was, for him, an inescapable site of toil.

And that's where I came in, and where all the others like me have continued to come in since. Every time I go back to visit my old friend Rob, I encounter a young version of myself. She, or sometimes he, can be found living in the trailer I used to live in and dispensing the same kind of careful conversation, alongside beer, espresso, pizza, and shots of Fireball. But no matter what they're doing (fetching kegs from Clallam Bay, cleaning the bathrooms, stocking the walk-in cooler), I know the truth: they're mostly there to listen, to keep Rob and the locals company, to be an envoy of cheer and distraction. They're there, in other words, to hang out, whether they like it not.

Professional conferences, it must be said, are not third places, though they exist apart from first and second places. They are not third places because they present strict barriers to inclusion: a person has to be accepted first (some conferences are very exclusive and operate as invitation-only; others, meanwhile, still require would-be attendees to apply and submit their work for approval); then that person has to pay, or get their institution or company to pay for them; then there is the social navigation of the conference scene itself, a process that, as the stories I have been telling here illustrate, can prove daunting and difficult.

But conferences, I think, aspire to a sort of third-place functionality, and that is part of what makes them so useful and necessary to those of us who depend on them for professional and intellectual growth. They take us away from both our places of work and our places of home, exploding the boundaries of our accustomed domestic and professional containers and forcing us to confront new challenges, ideas, and personalities. They also grant us some breathing space by placing us at a distance from the customer service imperative.

The requirement to hang out on the job—under duress, in the face of that specter known as "customer satisfaction"—is a byproduct of a cultural obsession with dwelling in isolation. The drive to dwell results in self-imposed separation and, by extension, in the compensatory need for paid human companionship. This makes hanging out on the job a required part of, in fact, *most* modern jobs, because it entitles the customer, who is the purchaser of someone else's labor power and time, to expectations of amiability. That customer is paying not just for whatever good, service, or product is being dispensed, but likewise for the manner in which it is dispensed. Customer service, especially in American culture, thus carries a mandate of forced friendliness. Without that mandate in place, the customer starts to feel that they have been robbed of the full value of the exchange and, next time, might just be better off staying home.

Most academics, it must be remembered, are also teachers. And it is through teaching that, increasingly, the customer service imperative asserts itself. Hanging out on the job, when the job takes place inside a college classroom and before a live audience of student-consumers who are paying far too much for the privilege of being there, means constantly being asked to compensate for the consumer's sacrifices—an impossible task. As the price of a college degree in America continues to climb, so do the expectations of professors' customer service skills. It is not enough to profess knowledge, to model insight gained through research, to design educational curricula, to evaluate students' work, and to provide intellectual mentorship. One must also be nice, and inspirational, and fun—enough to make up for everything that the consumer loses (money, time) just by being there. One must make up for the deprivations of a culture that is obsessed not just with productivity but with dwelling.

Walter Benjamin locates the origins of modern "dwelling" in the early part of the nineteenth century, an era that saw the compartmentalization of social life as people fled rural environs in search of factory jobs located in cities. And just as the factory, with its divisions and its specialized machinery and its assembly lines, divided up and cordoned off individual tasks requisite to the processes of "making," so did apartments (originally called *tenements*) enforce new standards of division and alienation within the domestic sphere. This focus on individualized space led, first, to a concomitant focus on the self and interiority (as seen in the rise of fields like psychology) and, second, to a mania for decorating and outfitting interior spaces. Think of the Victorian parlor, with its busy wallpaper and its knickknacks and its overstuffed furniture and potted ferns: "To live in these interiors," Benjamin observes, writing in the early part of the twentieth century, "was to have woven a dense fabric about oneself, to have secluded oneself within a spider's web, in whose toils world events hang loosely suspended like so many insect bodies sucked dry. From such a cavern, one does not like to stir."[10] Benjamin was noticing a connection between interiors, interiority, and a generalized retreat from the public sphere. People no longer gathered publicly to discuss news and politics; they went home to read about news and politics on their own (the first tenements in New York City were constructed in 1840 and *The New York Times* started publishing in 1851).

Oscar Wilde, that famous chronicler and critic of Victorian morals, would go on to observe something very similar decades later. Wilde's 1889 work "The Decay of Lying" reads like a satirical, modern take on the Socratic dialogue. It features two characters, one of whom, Cyril, invites the other to go on a walk outside. His companion, Vivian, refuses, complaining that "Nature is so uncomfortable . . . and filled with dreadful black insects." He tells his friend,

I prefer houses to the open air. Inside our houses, we all feel of the proper proportions; everything in sight is subordinated to us, fashioned for our uses and pleasures. Egotism itself, which is so necessary to a proper sense of human dignity, is entirely the result of indoor life.[11]

Vivian's observation—that egotism and selfishness are indispensable aspects of "human dignity," and that egotism can only be cultivated inside one's home or private dwelling—compares to Benjamin's. For, in Victorian culture, by the close of the nineteenth century, egotism had started to look like a viable replacement for feelings of dignity and self-satisfaction. The modern laborer, in no longer being able to take pride in his work, which was alienated through the industrial division of labor, had instead learned to take pride in his possessions.

Wilde's Vivian, in this fictional dialogue, mocks a familiar yet unspoken truth about modern life: that there is great comfort to be found in great narcissism. Benjamin picks up on this point, too, when he delves deeper into the meaning of the verb "to dwell." As Benjamin argues in his landmark work *The Arcades Project*, "*to dwell* is a transitive verb . . . it has to do with fashioning a shell for one's self." And, of course, while a shell provides necessary protection, its chief feature lies in its ability to conform precisely to the shape of the dweller. "The original form of all dwelling is existence not in the house but in the shell," Benjamin observes, "and the shell bears the impression of its occupant."[12] Another way of saying this—of summing up both Benjamin's and Wilde's anxieties about dwelling—is this: we like our houses and private spaces because they look like us; we fear public spaces because they are uncomfortable and different, because they don't look like us, and because, most terrifyingly, they force us to reckon with the realities of anonymity and numerousness. Being in public forces us to confront the fact that we might not be as exceptional as we thought.

The philosopher Theodor Adorno, a close associate of Walter Benjamin, lived to experience the results of a century's worth of forced isolation, social alienation, and rampant narcissism. Adorno was born a German Jew at the end of the nineteenth century; he saw Hitler come to power via popular vote; and, in 1941, he was forced to flee Germany for the United States. Once there, however, he observed conditions of isolation and aloofness that made him worry: post-war American culture looked, to his eye, too much like pre-war Germany. The post-war "baby boom" had resulted in the growth of the American suburbs, sprawling sections of land developed for first-place functionality (private residence) and located within commuting distance to second-place nuclei (cities, office buildings, places of work). Adorno watched Americans shuttle back and forth in their cars between work and home, and he critiqued what he saw as ever-deepening habits consistent with conditions of social alienation. "He who stands aloof runs the risk of believing himself better than others and misusing his critique of society as an ideology for his private interest," Adorno argues in his 1951 work *Minima Moralia*.[13] In other words, Adorno says, isolation begets feelings of superiority, but not solely because the isolated individual lacks opportunities for comparison; rather, isolation begets superiority because the isolated individual has no *audience* but himself, no one to receive (and, perhaps, critique) his image of himself, to test whether or not it is even accurate.

A conference is an invitation to engagement with a certain kind—a curated kind—of audience. It is also an excuse to hang out with that audience, to see conversations grow beyond the manicured spaces of a guarded professionalism. Sometimes, that results in activities, or in kinds of hanging out, that are pursued with predation in mind. I am not here to give those activities a pass; my own experiences have allowed me to see how traumatic they can be. And fortunately, many organizations, including those with which I am professionally allied, have recently begun to take steps to curtail or prevent such behaviors. The MLA, for example, did this when it opted to move past the era of interviews held in hotel rooms, which sometimes meant that candidates had to sit on beds while facing down ranks of interviewers seated before them in chairs. That the MLA has made this move despite anticipating how it will cost them in overall conference attendance is a sign that people are still interested in taking care of each other, even in a profession that is famous for predation and for the encouragement of cutthroat competition.

So while a conference might not constitute a third place, not fully, it nonetheless qualifies as an occasion for hanging out and, possibly, now and then, as a site of collective care. Indeed, it was at a conference a few years back that I first started to think seriously about hanging out. I was in New Orleans for the occasion; I spoke on a panel with my friend Robert, who I know from my time in graduate school; we were joined by a professional acquaintance of mine who, though we had corresponded, I had never met in person before. Together, that acquaintance and I ended up doing some hanging out and exploring the city, touring one of its historic cemeteries and wandering through the French Quarter. And besides these colleagues—one of them old, one of them new—I discovered that I recognized almost all of the other conference attendees, or many of them, anyway. In the space of a few years, I had gone from being invisible and anonymous, from occupying the shadows of the hotel bar, dreading interactions in the elevators, and sobbing in my hotel room because of a misunderstanding that was never, in fact, a misunderstanding, to finding myself somewhere near an epicenter of professional social activity.

Others, I know, cannot claim the privileges that have made such inclusion possible for me. They have been blocked—by the precariousness of their own working situations, by institutional austerity and greed, or else by a boss's suspicion that fun doesn't deserve to be funded. This means that whatever scene I am now likely to find myself in when I'm hanging out at a conference is a compromised one, and also one that is getting worse and more unequal every day. It is a scene, in other words, that cannot last, even though it needs to—even though I need it to. The fight for hanging out is the fight for inclusive access to scenes and places like the ones I have been describing. And it starts with recognizing that hanging out at, or around, or in the context of work is, in essence, work.

6

DINNER PARTIES

AS

HANGING OUT

There are good dinner parties and there are bad ones. The bad ones, I find, never really end: they stick with us, to the point where we catch ourselves wincing over the memories of them years and years hence. The good ones, though, they slip away from us, like water running downhill. We try to bring them back, grasping at the air after they are gone. That's how we know they were good in the first place.

Sometimes, we try to resuscitate them. I used to have a friend, a man named Émile, who owned a café in downtown Pittsburgh, a place I used to hang out. It was a stuffy little spot with too few customers and very good, very rich espresso: Émile had strong opinions about how things ought to be done and could not tolerate the thought of compromise. I went there for the view of Market Square and also for Émile and his stories. He liked to tell one about a dinner party he had attended many years before, in France.

This would have been in the 1980s. He was sort of bumming around back then, frequenting various towns along the southern coast, and he met a local girl and they started to hang around together. She invited him to dine one evening with her parents. The day of the dinner party came and he and the girl spent it at the beach and then they had to stop off to buy wine on the way to her parents' house. Émile didn't have a car, only a bike, and the girl didn't even have that much, so they took off from the beach with her on his handlebars.

When he got to this part in the story, Émile would always make a motion with his hand to describe their movements as they rolled up and over the hills toward the town. It was like he was caressing the shapes of the remembered terrain. The town, as he explained, would appear, bobbing there on the horizon, and then disappear again as the bike descended the next hill. Up and over. Now you see it, now you don't. He had to bike hard and the whole way, the girl's long, blonde hair kept flying back into his face and it would get in his mouth, which tickled and made him laugh.

At the market, the girl picked out the wine: it was sunset-colored, more orange than red or pink. Émile had never heard of the type and, afterward, he could never manage to conjure up its name again. At her parents' house, they opened the wine and had it alongside a first course of braised leeks in mustard sauce and it was the most glorious thing Émile had ever tasted, he said. The wine was sharp and dry and acidic, but also laced with honey. It was like the whole day at the beach had been boiled down and put into a bottle and then served cold, still smelling of all its good, warm summer smells.

Years later, back in Pittsburgh, Émile chanced upon the same wine for sale in a shop. He'd been looking for it for years but hadn't known what to ask for. He recognized it immediately, though, from the label and also the orange color, and he bought a bottle to take home and then picked up some leeks and whole grain mustard to go with it. But, as he would always tell it to me, when he tasted it all those years later, he realized it wasn't the wine, it had never been the wine. Rather, it had been "the flavor of the whole day," as he used to put it—that was what he had been tasting back then. It was brewed, that flavor, from a complex assortment of impressions, the beach and the bike ride and the girl and her hair in his mouth and her family's second-floor apartment with its windows open to the street and the leeks in mustard sauce and then also, finally, the wine. But it had never been just the wine.

I turn to the food writer M.F.K. Fisher when I want to think about what it means to cook and eat food in the company of others. Fisher is, so far as I am concerned, one of the preeminent twentieth-century voices not just on the subject of eating but on eating socially. This is ironic, perhaps, given that she is also the author of a famous essay about the joys of eating alone. Yet I view these vicissitudes of hers as representative of a larger and more holistic approach to what it means to treat the eating of food as a social occasion. It's a contradiction that, for me, also calls to mind the work of Ralph Waldo Emerson. Though famous for his views on self-reliance and solitude, Emerson nonetheless explores the meaning of friendship in an essay of that very title, observing how "the soul environs itself with friends, that it may enter into a grander self-acquaintance or solitude; and it goes alone, for a season, that it may exalt its conversation or society."[1] As Emerson sees it, there is a give and take, a push and pull. A friend comes into view, appears there on the horizon like that town Émile kept biking toward in the south of France, and then that friend disappears again, ducking down behind the hill.

It is this on-and-off character that binds fruitful solitude to social activity, according to Emerson. Though seemingly diametrically opposed, the two activities actually occur in conjunction, strengthening each other like a set of complementary muscle groups. In a similar way, I see Fisher's writing about food as a series of social excursions into the larger world of eating, launched in the company of like-minded people. That give and take, or ideological balance, is there even when she is writing about eating alone. In fact, as she sees it, eating alone can provide necessary preparation for dining well and comfortably in the presence of others. The problem is that the lonesome diner often fails to realize that when they are dining alone, they are not really dining alone, "they are dining with themselves."[2] This constitutes something of a missed opportunity because in dining with one's self, Fisher argues, a person may well discover "time to look about him; quiet in which to savor his present mouthful; opportunity to broil his steak in a new way."[3] These skills, which are honed in private, may then be put to good use the next time an opportunity for companionship presents itself.

Throughout her many books, Fisher's stories and impressions unfurl as naturally as conversation does at a good, comfortable dinner party—that is, without program or structure and with plenty of topical detours that, somehow, always lead back to a soft, sunlit patch of common ground. And though she must have experienced her fair share of them, Fisher almost never writes about bad dinner parties. Instead, she maintains a charitable outlook and chooses to focus her attention on memories of good ones. She presents them invitingly and then adds in a colorful garnish or two in the form of warnings, advice, or light kitchen humor. She does not lecture to her reader, though she, like my old friend Émile, is never short on opinions and has plenty to say about how things should be done.

This is especially true of the essays in her 1942 *How to Cook a Wolf.* The contents of this collection, which is one of Fisher's more celebrated titles, emerge from the depths of World War II. They are accordingly marked by the bleakness of a background they can neither fully comprehend nor ignore. There is rationing; there is hardship; there are never enough eggs or butter; instead, there is "War Cake," a dreary but serviceable concoction made from shortening and other shelf-stable alternatives to those more desired ingredients. And at the end of the collection, rounding out the whole thing, is an essay detailing what Fisher would eat if only she could, if only it weren't for the war. It is an invitation for the reader to dwell, just for a minute, within the fold of delicious fantasy or, as Fisher puts it, to "sit back in your chair . . . Drop a few years from your troubled mind. Let the cupboard of your thoughts fill itself with a hundred ghosts that long ago . . . used to be easy to buy and easy to forget."[4]

It's a gorgeous essay, a heartbreaking essay. It is full of warmth and yet bracketed on all sides by suffering: only a year before writing it, a recently divorced Fisher had lost her lover, the illustrator George Dillwyn Parrish, to suicide. As she wrote *How to Cook a Wolf*, she was alone and without even butter or eggs to comfort her. I read this final essay, which is called "How to Practice True Economy," for the first time in the spring of 2021, about one year into the COVID-19 pandemic, and I cried and thought about dinner parties. Recently, I read it again and thought about what it was like to read it the year before, and I cried thinking about how I had cried that first time.

Fisher's approach to this essay, and to all the others in the collection, is a seductive one because it rests on unshakable faith about the future. The war would end, of course; the butter and eggs would return. Fisher knew this, believed this, and in her essays, you can feel that knowledge throbbing beneath the layers of practical advice about, say, how to make meat drippings last for a week. Fisher never doubted that there would be dinners worth eating in the future, and dinner *parties* worth lingering over in good company. Her dogged belief in future pleasures did not leave her much room to despair for the present, or even the recent and very tragic past.

If a party offers an opportunity for exuberance—an occasion to listen in on the whole, rowdy symphony that is human social life and to hear it played at the highest possible volume—then a dinner party is its quieter cousin, something closer to a chamber music suite or a piano sonata. Dinner parties are about intimacy, as opposed to exuberance. They're also about fantasy.

The food magazine *Bon Appétit*, for instance, has for years featured a column that asks celebrities to wax euphoric on the subject of their "dream dinner party." These celebrity interviewees have to name three famous people, living or dead, who would form the social nexus of the imagined event. The results tend to fall somewhere between curious and abhorrent, depending on the interviewee's tastes. The politician Stacey Abrams, for instance, opts for an interesting but, one can only imagine, awkward conversational mix: her dream dinner party includes the science fiction writer Octavia E. Butler, former president Lyndon B. Johnson, and the *Star Trek* character Captain Kathryn Janeway.[5] Note that Abrams names the character, not the actress, Kate Mulgrew, who played Captain Janeway. This detail would appear to underline her own interest in the whole "fantasy" component.

Others interviewees, meanwhile, prefer to keep things rooted in some vision of reality, albeit a historically rosy one. The writer and television producer (and baron and conservative member of England's House of Lords) Julian Fellowes, for example, selects his own dining room at his ancestral estate in Dorset as the setting of his dream dinner party. "We'd use the china with the family crest and turquoise trim, and the room would be lit with silver candlesticks," he explains. Fellowes prioritizes such scenic details over other considerations in a way that rather recalls his work on famed television series like *Downton Abbey* and *The Gilded Age*. The point in both cases, it would seem, is not what happens or who is involved, but how it all looks and gets aesthetically organized. Accordingly, Fellowes's first pick for a fantasy guest is an aesthetically pleasing one: the actress Marilyn Monroe. Fellowes justifies this choice by describing Monroe's talent for appearing "needy" and enlisting "the viewer's help"—characteristics, it seems, that might make other dinner party attendees feel more confident and relaxed. Like the beautiful china and silver candlesticks, Fellowes seems to include her for the sake of having something exquisite to look at, something that, in being likewise vulnerable, can be trusted not to challenge others or dominate conversation. Fellowes's other dream guests include Ella Fitzgerald, "my all-time favorite singer," and the novelist Anthony Trollope, which he explains by noting, "I'm president of the Trollope Society."[6] (As for me, I'd sooner eat my own foot than attend this particular nightmare of a dinner party.)

With both Abrams and Fellowes, then, we see that the idea of the dream dinner party is, often, a fantasy concocted along the lines of fandom. Both interviewees are celebrities in their own right, yet they dream of what it might mean to intimately gather in the presence of people whose celebrity outranks theirs. Seen in this way, dinner parties are not just about intimacy but about *aspirational* forms of intimacy, in particular. It's one thing to find oneself at a crowded party with a famous celebrity in attendance; it's another thing to face that person in private, across the space of a dinner table. To dream of such an encounter is to dream of getting a famous person alone, or nearly alone, and on intimate terms. It is the dream of having their undivided attention, or else of giving them yours, of settling in to hear the stories they reserve for close friends, the ones that flip a switch on a secret spotlight and show you who they are when they are not pretending to be the person who everyone else believes them to be. That dream leans heavily on expectations about authenticity. How can one be expected to feel the same way about a person after bearing witness to how they cut a steak, or eat spaghetti, or handle a raw oyster, let alone a complicated salad?

The dream dinner party grows out of the more commonplace fantasies that structure even the most humble of gatherings, I think. We like to ask questions about what it would mean to be on close, familiar terms with people we admire, to see them do average things like work their way around a bowl of soup, because to do that necessitates envisioning how that person might operate if they were placed beside us, on our own level. With that fantasy comes the dream of thinking that, perhaps, at heart, that famous person already is on our level—that they are just like us or, even more importantly, that *we* are just like them.

I'm interested in dinner parties on account of all that dream scaffolding. It's what drives me to ask questions about them. What makes for a good one, for instance? What causes a bad one to swerve off course? How did dinner parties become the narrative bedrock that supports so many different genres of storytelling in our culture, from romantic comedies to horror movies to classic nineteenth-century "big house" novels? And why dinner, in particular? Is it because of that meal's temporal placement, at the end of the long day, after traditional working hours have elapsed?

I think that's certainly part of it. But in my experience, the seductions and promises of a dinner party are primarily to be found in the low costs of entry. A person doesn't need to be particularly good at anything in order to enjoy herself a dinner party: no special skills are required outside of the skill of eating, which is about as basic as it gets, and perhaps the skill of talking. You just need to be able, and willing, to hang out—to kill time, in other words, though that is a turn of phrase that Fisher warns us against. "If time, so fleeting, must like humans die, let it be filled with good food and good talk," Fisher argues, "and then embalmed in the perfumes of conviviality."[7] I take this as a gloss on the old adage that anything worth doing is worth doing well. If dinner must be had, then it might as well be had under agreeable terms, and in agreeable—if not necessarily "dream"—company.

A dinner party, then, is an invitation to experience intimacy, but also a reminder that intimacy can actually be obtained through pretty humble means.

As with all parties, dinner parties are about time and the taking of it. And because time is a commodity in our modern world—an "object of human want,"[8] in the words of philosopher John Stuart Mill, meaning a thing that is desired and fought over within a sphere of competition deemed a "market"—it is not something that can be taken for granted as being universally accessible. As with all commodities, time gets unevenly distributed across the range of income brackets. Those existing at one end of that range, the ones with a lot of money, can afford to have more of it. This is because they are able to pay others to perform services and tasks that would, otherwise, take their time away from them. Meanwhile, those at the other end of the range, the ones who are forced to perform those services and tasks, wind up shielding and consecrating the time of that other, more fortunate population. They sell their labor and their time to them, the more resource-rich. In exchange, they receive the wages that allow them to purchase goods and services for themselves. But they do not receive time, since time *is* money to those who find themselves continually forced to work for it.

This means that dinner parties, as leisure activities, are underpinned by assumptions of privilege. Taking the time to loiter over a multi-course meal, to enjoy and savor an activity that has mere routine sustenance as its real end, is an inherently classed pursuit. It is classed, in fact, to the very same degree as one's ability to pay for all those multiple courses. Everyone, or most everyone, eats dinner, but only some can lay claim to the time and resources that are necessary to elevate the act of eating dinner to the status of a what is called a "party," meaning a celebratory occasion that is organized around the pursuit of pleasure itself.

In a short film from 2008 called *Next Floor,*[9] by the Canadian director Denis Villeneuve (since made more famous by his work on films like *Dune*), a group of elite guests gathers for a dinner party that escalates into carnage. The guests' affluence is clear from their style of dress and from the way that they are attended by a swarm of white-coated waitstaff. Throughout the whole film, which is only about ten minutes long, they never leave their seats, in fact— because they don't have to. They also don't speak. Theirs is a dinner party without conversation, where all the attention is directed

toward the garish display of dishes laid before them on a long banquet table. Meat dishes, served raw and seeping, figure prominently
among them. The aesthetics of slaughter and animal viscera are
heightened by the film's repeated use of the color red: red cherries
line the edges of an oily pork roast, red wine fills the guests' glasses,
and red lipstick glares like an open wound on the mouth of a pale-
faced matriarch seated at the head of the table.

About three minutes into the film, the meaning of its title is
made clear as the banquet table, groaning under the weight of all
those many dishes, goes crashing through the floor, along with the
guests who are seated around it. The waitstaff, and the four members of a string quartet, are left behind, looking curiously unper-
turbed; a head waiter uses an intercom to announce "Next floor,"
and the staff and string quartet go rushing downstairs to attend
to the dinner guests in their now slightly altered, slightly more
disheveled surroundings. The chandelier, even, gets lowered down
on a pulley. The guests pause for a moment and take stock of the
changes. The meat is now covered in a fine film of plaster dust and
so are their faces, hands, and clothing. The waitstaff comes around
with feather dusters to remove the detritus from the guests' shoulders. Then the string quartet strikes up again and the whole action
of the dinner resumes, with the guests helping themselves to additional cuts of the now thoroughly begrimed meat.

New courses are wheeled in at this point. With the dinner party's
demotion of one floor, the fare has grown more vulgar and explicit.
Whole carcasses of animals are put on display, complete with faces
and fur, their backs split open to reveal choice cuts. There is an
armadillo, a mountain lion, a rhinoceros, even. The guests show no
hint of surprise or offense as they slice into the backs, stomachs,

or flanks of these animals or select the parts that are offered on silver trays. They can barely settle into this new parade of slaughter, though, before the floor begins to creak and, once again, they are sent crashing through it to land one floor below.

Here the sense of routine becomes apparent, as the staff scrambles to repeat the motions that they carried out on the previous floor. Again there comes the announcement on the intercom, "Next floor," and again the cellist from the string quartet, along with everyone else, goes bumping down the stairs. But this time, the guests don't have time, even, to relax into eating before they are demoted once more. The whole process gets repeated over and over, until the guests end up crashing through multiple floors at once, sailing through an endless succession of them as they careen toward their final stop, a concrete-floored basement. The chandelier, which has reached the end of its tether, plummets after them, disappearing down into the darkness. The staff and string quartet are left staring down into the hole that has been left by the greedy, pampered guests.

The film then ends right where it began: with a long close-up on the face of the head waiter. It is entirely devoid of feeling, that face. Its blankness echoes that of the black hole that has swallowed the dinner party guests. It is the mask of a person whose whole career has been built on the practiced suppression of emotion. It stares down the camera, backed by a crescendo of what sound like war drums. It refuses to feel or see. It radiates the dispassion that is the hallmark of hospitality and good service.

What the film *Next Floor* illustrates is, to begin with, the carnage wrought by class inequality. One group dines, engaging in a frenzied consumption of resources (and lives, since all of the dishes are made from meat), while the other looks on and labors on their behalf. One group takes its time; the other gives it. The film uses a signature experience of upper-class life, a dinner party, to symbolize the bottomless pit that is elite consumption under commodity capitalism.

In doing so, it enters into dialogue with other, similar depictions of class inequality that have surfaced throughout history. It brings to mind, for instance, the so-called "Pyramid of Capitalist System,"[10] which is an illustrated work of propaganda published by the Industrial Workers of the World (IWW) and first circulated via that organization's official magazine, the *Industrial Worker*, beginning in 1911. The image, though, did not originate with the IWW, who took inspiration from similar versions that had previously circulated in countries like Belgium and Russia. The illustration shows the various social and economic classes arranged within a pyramid. At the top of the pyramid is an assortment of governmental leaders, including both kings and democratically elected rulers like the American president. In fact, in the IWW's version, the president figure, who appears on the top left, bears a striking resemblance to President William Howard Taft, who was in office at the time of the poster's creation. He holds a top hat in one hand and sports a handlebar moustache along with parted hair that falls just to the left of center, as Taft's own hair did. In fact, the image might be taken for a composite of Taft and his predecessor, President Theodore Roosevelt, who wore his hair and moustache in an almost identical fashion, thereby reinforcing the idea that the two men are effectively the same (Roosevelt designated Taft as his own successor and, as a result, Taft received little opposition in his bid for the presidency in 1908).

In envisioning the structure of capitalist society as rigidly pyrami-
dal, the illustration draws attention to the fact that most people living
under capitalism fall at the bottom. Indeed, the larger an economic
class is, and the more numerous its members, the further down it
is positioned. Very few, for example, can claim status at the top as
rulers. The second-to-largest class, meanwhile, positioned one rung
up from the bottom, is the bourgeoisie, the group of property owners and managers who exist beneath rulers and clerics, for example,
but nonetheless possess the privilege of having things to sell that are
not limited to their raw muscle, labor power, or time. This group of
people is depicted in a state of leisure, enjoying—you guessed it—a
dinner party. Alongside them is a caption: "We eat for you."

As the second-to-largest class, the bourgeoisie is shown propped
up by the largest one, which is the working class. In the illustration,
this most common sector of the population appears to bend under
the weight of all the other classes that it is forced, though the sale
of its labor, to support. Children number among the ranks of those
who bear the burden of all that labor (recall that we're talking about
the year 1911 and laws restricting child labor were not passed at the
federal level until 1938). One of them uses a shovel to reach what
her little arms cannot, which is the ceiling of her own class position,
made heavy and impenetrable by the mass of those above. Another
child, meanwhile, appears to have expired from the effort and lies
on the ground with her eyes closed, presumably dead. Next to these
figures who fill out the bottom rung of capitalist production, there
are two captions: "We work for all" and "We feed all."

The messages are not hard to locate in this illustration—indeed,
that is the whole point where propaganda is concerned. Rather, they
appear blasted at full volume. The bourgeoisie lounge on the pyra-

mid's second level wearing fine clothes, raising cocktail glasses to the sky and, in one figure's case, passed out upon the table, even. They are enjoying themselves while those below them are left to suffer and die. The bourgeoisie's enjoyment is leisurely, ample, and born from idleness. They do not have to work for the food that is the source of their enjoyment. There are others, lurking down below, who have been conscripted to do that for them.

These two documents—the "Pyramid of Capitalist System" and Villeneuve's short film *Next Floor*—offer criticisms aimed at the same target, which is a very old and very familiar one. Together, they both expose the logic of how some can want and go hungry while others indulge to the point of gross excess. And they both use the idea of a dinner party to represent those divisions in experience and suffering. In Villeneuve's *Next Floor*, the dinner guests do not need that which they consume. In fact, so great is the weight of all their excess that it breaks the system, so to speak, represented by the architecture of the building they are in, and sends them crashing down through the floor. Each time that happens, the laborers who have been paid to attend to them and their dinner party—the waitstaff and the members of the string quartet—are forced to descend with them, down one more floor, though they are not responsible for what has happened. The workers work, the indulgers indulge, and the whole thing keeps falling apart, suggesting a need for greater balance in the activities of the two populations.

All of this makes a devastating kind of sense when one stops to think about the year in which Villeneuve's *Next Floor* appeared: 2008. That was a year—though, tragically enough, hardly the *only* year—in which the cracks and fissures in our shared economic structures became obvious to the naked eye. That was the year those cracks got really big, really noticeable. That was the year they grew to swallow whole families, houses, livelihoods, and futures.

Were there dinner parties that year, in 2008? Of course there were. There always are. But there were also bank runs, unemployment claims, housing foreclosures, federal stimulus programs, and bailouts for the big banks that had helped start it all, the ones that were left floundering when homeowners started defaulting on their high-risk mortgages. Some had a lot back then, in 2008, because some always do. But some—a lot more—struggled to get by with very little. The dinner parties, meanwhile, raged on.

A little more than five years ago, I found myself at what ought to have been, by my standards, a dream dinner party.

There I was, seated between the science fiction writer Kim Stanley Robinson and the renowned physicist Brian Greene. Robinson is the author of speculative novels like *Aurora*, *New York 2140*, and *The Ministry for the Future*, to name just a few of my favorites (though, at the time, the first of these had just been published and the second was still in process). I'd spent the whole day with him, actually, because my partner, Dave, had been appointed to serve as Robinson's driver while he was visiting for our university's annual Writers Conference. Turned out, though, Robinson didn't require much chauffeuring; he had been content to hang out with Dave and me. The three of us had spent three hours comfortably occupying a corner booth at the café attached to our campus art museum, talking science fiction and the philosopher Fredric Jameson and other topics. That's where Robinson had told us about one of the characters in his upcoming novel, who was to be based on the science fiction writer Octavia E. Butler (one of Stacey Abrams's picks, you might recall, for her own dream dinner party, and my own former neighbor who lived across the street from my family when I was growing up).

I was also familiar with Greene's work, having been assigned, and awed by, *The Elegant Universe* back when I was in college. That night at dinner, I found myself in an unprecedented position— one that seemed to teeter on the verge of fantasy conditions. I was talking accordions with Robinson on one side and plant-based eating with Greene (who is actually vegan) on the other. This was in a private dining room at a restaurant called Sky's, which looked onto downtown Grand Forks from a vantage point of mahogany and leather interiors and top-shelf liquor. It was where we English faculty always went for meals with visiting authors, when we were allowed to go at all.

The Writers Conference dinners were invitation-only, see, and usually limited to about a dozen people, with half of the spots reserved for the visiting writers themselves. It was Dave's chauffeuring duties that had won us seats at this one, along with a bit of work on my part (some graphic design—flyers and buttons and promotional materials to advertise the event—plus, earlier that day, I'd moderated a panel discussion featuring both Robinson and Greene). Dave and I, we enjoyed these dinners and were always quick to claim our spots at them, when we were invited to do so. But we also dreaded them. This was because we had to pay for them ourselves and Sky's was the most expensive restaurant in town. The visiting writers' meals were covered by the university, but ours, as faculty, were not.

We were poor, Dave and I. We were living paycheck to paycheck, and sometimes not even able to succeed in doing that, clinging to the lifeline that is credit and deferred balances. Dave was teaching as an adjunct in the English department at the University of North Dakota, which meant he was earning about a few thousand dollars per class without benefits or health care. And I, meanwhile, hadn't received a substantive raise since moving to North Dakota several years before, owing to a pernicious cycle of state-legislated cuts to education budgets.

So we were always poor back then, poor enough to begrudge a thirty-dollar plate of walleye alongside a fifteen-dollar glass of wine, times two, and that was only if we got away easy, if we successfully avoided any conversation about appetizers or cocktails or desserts. With Robinson and Greene in attendance, though, there had been no question. We were going, and to hell with what the credit card statement said after. Because the thing about a dinner party is it only ever happens once in the exact way that it happens.

The conversation that evening went smoothly, save for periodic interruptions from a man seated across the table from me. This man was the chancellor of our university system and he had known Greene personally, or so he kept explaining to anyone who he might catch listening, decades before, back when they were both Rhodes scholars. He was going to be introducing Greene's big public lecture, which was scheduled to take place right after dinner. Two servers kept whisking in and out of our little private dining room, ferrying entrées or replacement glasses of wine. I recognized them both, of course, because that was the way of things in our little university town: one server was a recent graduate of our master's program in

English, a promising student who had returned to waiting tables as he contemplated his next move. The other was a current graduate student in that same program.

I had the walleye. I always had the walleye at Sky's. Dave had the other fish, whatever it was, probably salmon and probably over-cooked. The chancellor, sitting across from me, had filet mignon with multiple glasses of red wine. He seemed totally unaware of how this situation impeded his efforts to maintain conversation with his vegan friend across the table. At one point in the meal, the server asked the chancellor—who was not a regular at our confer-ences and was probably only there to score points with Greene—if he might like to simply order a whole bottle of wine instead of going it by the glass, always the more expensive way to do things. The chancellor looked at Dave and me and asked, with a laugh, "Who's paying for this anyway?"

I had thought it was a joke.

Greene and the chancellor had to take off early to prepare for the evening's lecture. That left Robinson, Dave, myself, and one or two others. Once again, the conversation was easy and energetic. Once again, I was mesmerized, unable to feel the minutes slipping by, which they continued to do until it was just the three of us again, like it had been all afternoon. It was then that one of the servers approached us.

I could see the worry lurking at the edges of his smile, like he was upset but trying not to be. One of the dinner party guests, he explained, had racked up a big bill and left without paying. He won-dered if my partner and I, if we might . . .

I mentioned that there are good dinner parties and there are bad ones. I mentioned that the bad ones have a tendency to stick with us, to insert themselves in our recollections and make general nuisances of themselves. This, for me, is one of them.

What started out as a dream dinner party ended with Dave and me paying for the chancellor's lavish dinner, on top of our own. It shouldn't have happened but, after all was said and done, it was the only thing that *could* happen, the only fair conclusion to the scenario. I couldn't let our server (who I knew was saving up to get the hell out of Grand Forks, his hometown) get stiffed on the tip that was due from the chancellor's bill. And I'd worked in enough restaurants to know what happens when someone skips out on a check, to know that it's the workers, not the owners, who suffer most directly in those cases. I thought back to the time I had spent working as a country club server in Ohio, at a restaurant that was much like Sky's, where everything was reliably overpriced and over-cooked. I thought about what it was like when someone failed to leave a tip for a giant party that took up the better part of my time and attention for over two hours and kept me from getting assigned to other tables. I thought about how little my regular wage (back then in Ohio, it was $2.15 an hour; today in North Dakota, some fifteen years later, it's still only $4.86 an hour) went toward making up for those losses. I thought about how the other servers would, begrudgingly, end up pooling and splitting *their* hard-won tips, how we would all be forced to fall back on a system that served no one fairly. And so I did what I had to do and I paid the bill and made sure the server got the tip he deserved.

In the years that followed, I would often recall that thwarted dream dinner party of ours, sometimes by choice and sometimes by compulsion. Little things would crop up and set my memory stirring and stewing. I might come across one of the books that Robinson had inscribed to us during his visit: *To Dave and Sheila, My North Dakota hosts—KSR*. But often, such reminders came courtesy of the chancellor's voice, which came snaking its way through radio frequencies to invade the space of our living room. In the fall of 2017, he was facing allegations of sexual harassment and gender-based discrimination,[11] and so was much in the news. All I could think, every time an NPR broadcast forced me to, was, *That guy owes me two hundred dollars.*

But, then, there are the good ones.

Because then there comes the taste of the whole long day, of the beach near Carry-le-Rouet (or whichever town my friend Émile had been bumming around back then), of the bicycle ride over the rolling hills, the little town playing hide-and-seek on the horizon, the girl and the flavor of her hair in his mouth, the braised leeks in mustard sauce, the wine that looked and tasted like a sunset. There were, or are, or continue to be these things, and sometimes we don't have to be rich in order to get up close to them, even.

In fact, if we keep reminding ourselves that a dinner party can be made from three pretty humble ingredients—time, people, and food—then we likewise remember that such things are easy to get at and come by. After all, a cookout is a dinner party. A backyard barbecue is a dinner party. A potluck in the park is a dinner party. A picnic with friends is a dinner party. A chili cook-off is a dinner party. A date, of the friendly variety or otherwise, is small sort of dinner party. A couple of takeout meals shared on a stoop, that's also a dinner party. So many things are, or have the potential to be, a dinner party, if only one has the will and the time to make them so. It doesn't matter if it happens at a table or on a couch (I spent the most of the year 2020 living in an apartment that was so small, it could only accommodate one or the other) or if it's spread out on a blanket on the ground.

One of my favorite dinner parties, for instance, happens once a year and always in a different place. The food at this dinner party tends to be bad, but it doesn't matter because food is beside the point where this occasion is concerned. What matters most, instead, is the company and the scenery, the "flavor of the whole day," as Émile might say.

Each August, I head off into the Cascade Mountains in the company of Dave, my dad, a man who I like to call my honorary uncle (who is actually my dad's best friend), his brothers, their offspring, plus a smattering of neighbors and former coworkers who are connected to this whole big party of ours. Usually, this breaks down to a group of about ten or twelve. It's always the Cascades because that is where the majority of the group is headquartered, in my dad's hometown of Snohomish, Washington, a little place that looks out across a valley at a big blue-and-white swathe of those very mountains. Each year, we meet up in Snohomish before dawn and then carpool to whatever trailhead my honorary uncle, Mac, has picked out for us. Then we get our gear together, hitch it up on our backs, and we climb and we climb, hauling whatever we need to get us through four or five days of the same.

Come evening, we arrive as a group at the place we were supposed to be going and that's where the dinner party happens. There's usually a body of water—a clear, cold mountain tarn, or a lake that glows teal in the sun, or sometimes just a river tumbling off a nearby cliff and kicking up a companionable racket. In pairs, we set to the work of preparing our various meals, with names on packaging giving us cues about flavors we're supposed to be hunting for by the time the rehydrated stuff ends up in our mouths. This is true of all of us except John and Candace, who are camp gourmets. They are the ones who taught me how to pack herbs like basil and tarragon so that they'll keep fresh over several days and also how to carry eggs up a mountain, because a nice egg, soft-poached in boiling water over a camp stove, is handy meal booster. We never have wine to go with our meals because the bottles would be too heavy. Sometimes we have whiskey, but even when we don't, or when the first night's enthusiasm causes us to run out of it too quickly, we have other sedatives.

We have the high, still mountain air, which, particularly on the eastern slope of the Cascades, grows tawny as the day tilts toward dusk. We have our exhaustion and all the miles we've already sweated now behind us. We have each other and a good year's worth of conversation to catch up on. And, most importantly, we don't have anything else: no screens to divert our attention when the conversation lags, nowhere else to be, no concerns apart from sore muscles and maybe the search for ground that is flat enough to accommodate a tent. Sometimes it rains and we hunker down and project our conversations through tent walls, searching each other out. Sometimes it's clear and warm and perfect and we sit in a circle with our backs propped against logs or trees or our empty packs. And sometimes the bugs are too bad, or the ashes from nearby forest fires, and the dinner party ends early in the hopes of better conditions to follow on the next night.

I love this dinner party, which happens on repeat for about four or five nights in a row each year. I make a lot of sacrifices—plane tickets, scheduled vacations, cat-sitters, not to mention the burden of enduring multiple cross-country flights in hiking boots—in order to secure my annual place at it. And I never regret the cost, though the climb can be arduous, the weather punishing, and, sometimes, when we emerge from the mountains via the wrong trailhead, I'm the one who gets stuck with the responsibility of flagging down a stranger's car and hitchhiking back to the right one. (I have done this, quite recently, and it took a lot of crying to convince the person to let me ride with them—another sacrifice, of dignity in this particular case.) But each time I do it, I know that I'm seizing one more link on a finite chain of possible moments. The oldest members of our little party are in their seventies. We will not be able to do this forever, so we have to do it now, to the best of our abilities. For "When shall we live, if not now?" asks Fisher.[12] She is paraphrasing the stoic philosopher Seneca here, yet she is asking what is perhaps the most important rhetorical question about time of all time. When shall we seize and take that time for ourselves, if not in the short space of time that is to be found in a day—in this day, perhaps?

It was one the members of this hiking party of ours, Mac's brother, Andy, who first guided me to Fisher and her writing, in fact. We were hiking the Pacific Crest Trail and stopped overnight at a beautiful, high mountain cirque, which is like a mountainous amphitheater that guards a lake. In this case, it was Lake Sally Ann that was being held inside the circle of those granite cliffs, which rang with the whistling calls of marmots. There, we settled in and pitched our tents on a grassy platform positioned just above the lake and got our second night's dinner party-going. From his bag, Andy pulled the book that he had brought with him for the trip, a paperback copy of *How to Cook a Wolf.* He explained that its author was a favorite food writer of his, and I remember commenting on his ability to read about gourmet cooking and thoughtfully prepared meals when he was so far from anything resembling either. That's when he started explaining about how the book is about food but really, and more significantly, about the lack of it, about learning to "live most agreeably in a world full of an increasing number of disagreeable surprises," in Fisher's words.[13] When we emerged from the woods and I landed back in Seattle some days later, I went straight to one of my favorite bookstores, Third Place Books, to pick up a copy. And at the little mountain dinner party that was to follow the year after (that next time, in a high, glacial gully slung between Mt. Adams and Mt. Rainier, a hundred or so miles south of Lake Sally Ann), Andy and I would spend much of it discussing Fisher.

At these annual occasions, I have eaten things that go by many names. I have eaten that which calls itself red beans and rice, chana masala, mushroom stroganoff, and fettuccini alfredo (not recommended, by the way). I have eaten gallons of the pure, flavorless fuel that is instant oatmeal. I have sipped concoctions both holy and unholy—chamomile tea made from filtered pond water, with pine needles suspended like croutons on its surface; instant coffee tasting of the dregs of whatever my cup last held, usually oatmeal; a cocktail made from bourbon and Tang (surprisingly not bad). I have also eaten mountain huckleberries off the bush, and salmonberries at their peak of ripeness, and mere specks of blueberries that somehow pack five times the flavor of anything that can be found seven thousand feet below.

I have tasted good things and bad, in other words, though the individual flavors of those things, much like Émile's wine, were never the point. What has mattered, each time, is the work of collective arrival—taking the time to get to a place where time itself feels different, and to arrive there all together, in the company of people I care about. Kim Stanley Robinson, also an avid backpacker, describes that feeling of collective arrival as "re-entering a miracle."[14] It is a phrase that evokes the feeling of entering into something known and familiar, marked by generations of ritualistic occurrence, that yet persists in feeling incessantly new. And it is the caring that makes the flavor of the whole day happen. It is the seizing of a moment that you hope will come again, but which is really only here right now, that proves to be the true source of satiation.

HANGING OUT

ON THE

INTERNET

Not long after I moved to Vermont, I met a man who does not have an email address. I was looking to purchase bulk quantities of honey and a colleague directed me to the man in question, who is something of a local legend. Not only does he not have an email address, he's never had one, though he does maintain a website in support of his honey business. It lists information about his beekeeping practices along with a phone number and PO box and invites potential customers to call or send letters.

I called. The man, Kirk, had honey for sale by the gallon.

I kept getting hung up on the detail about the email address, though. This was in 2020 and I had just moved across the United States—during a pandemic, no less—to begin a new job that I had applied for, received an offer for, then negotiated and accepted *over the internet*. I had toured apartments *over the internet*. I had signed contracts that bound me to certain conditions of employment and residence *over the internet*. I had sent a security deposit and first month's rent to my new landlord *over the internet*. And, once I arrived in Vermont, I was to discover that, due to the complications of the ongoing pandemic, I would have to spend the ensuing school year teaching exclusively *over the internet*. How was it possible, I wondered, that my life could be structured in such a way—that it could be so thoroughly dependent on the infrastructural mesh of all that invisible technology—while, just miles down the road from me, there lived a man who lacked even the ability to send an email? How could it be that he and I were residents of the same time period, let alone universe?

I was born in the mid-eighties and the internet arrived on scene for most of us in the mid-nineties, around 1992 or 1993. What this means is that it has mostly always been there for me, as it has for others of my generation. However, our collective outlook has been, according to many, defined by the fact that we can still remember a time before that was true. I got my first email address in 1995, when I was twelve. But I will admit to being slow at adopting the rest of the accessories and habits that came with the shift to a digital lifestyle, most of which started to intensify when smartphones debuted in 2007. It took me almost another decade to make that particular shift. As a result, I didn't start to hang out on the internet in earnest until I was already in my thirties.

As someone who more or less came of age with the internet, I have often felt that I ought to be more adept at hanging out on, or in, or with it. I'm still not sure, even, which preposition works to best describe the amorphous situatedness that comes from those kinds of interactions. But I have never been able to reconcile the feeling of leaving behind a physical world in the name of nurturing more intense commitments to a virtual one. Indeed, when I first heard about Kirk, the local beekeeper with no email address, my reaction came not via words but physical sensation. I felt a sharp pang of jealousy tear through me with the force of a projectile. *How come I have to live on the internet and he doesn't?* was the question that seemed to throb in its wake.

At first, when I started hanging out on the internet, I blamed my doing so on North Dakota. I was new in a place that valued its solitude, one that insisted on placing spatial buffers between people. I had believed it was the twin specters of space and distance that caused me to turn to the internet and, at long last, to the strain of digital activity—meaning social media—that I'd spent years avoiding. But I've since come to understand that this move of mine probably had less to do with place and more to do with time. At thirty-one years old, I had reached, in a somewhat delayed fashion, the age of loneliness, which is another way of saying that I had reached adulthood itself. Whereas my twenties had felt like an almost effortlessly social time, a situation that was helped by the fact that I had spent much of it in cities, my thirties had appeared on the horizon looking a lot like the North Dakota landscape. There were wide open spaces to be found there, laid out beneath sprawling skies, and here and there a little hive of activity—a town, a gathering, a party, a friend—tossing its shadow over what were, otherwise, bright vacancies of land.

The problem in a place like North Dakota comes from the way that a person tends to grow accustomed to all that space, to the point where they view vacancy as a selling point, not a problem. Outside of Fargo, for instance, there is a well-known billboard placed alongside I-29 that shows an image of that same highway cutting through a bare swathe of prairie under searing blue skies. In it, the highway appears empty of cars. The slogan atop the billboard, rendered in the state's official and vaguely tribal font, proclaims: NORTH DAKOTA . . . THE RUSH HOUR COMMUTE. I own a postcard version of this billboard, which I purchased shortly after moving to North Dakota and, presumably, with the intention of mailing it to someone who would enjoy the irony that is implicit in the state's efforts to sell emptiness as a virtue. The back of the postcard, meanwhile, makes the image's message even more explicit: "Looking for life with less clutter?" it reads, "Come to NORTH DAKOTA!!" The suggestion is that *humans* are the real "clutter." The prospect of an empty highway and an easy "rush hour commute" serves to instruct the viewer—who, if we're talking about the billboard, is already *in* North Dakota—that geographic and spatial vacancy can offer respite from the stress-inducing clutter of human companionship.

Wallace Stegner, one of the great writers of the prairie, observes how life there becomes structured around such expectations of emptiness. "The world is very large, the sky is even larger, and you are very small. But also the world is flat, empty, nearly abstract, and in its flatness you are a challenging upright thing, as sudden as an exclamation mark, as enigmatic as a question mark."[1] The same, I think, can be said of age. Whereas social proximity tends to come easily when we are young, it can start to thin out once a person reaches the open range of adulthood. And with enough time and practice, a person simply adapts, adjusting their eyes to the sparseness of their social surroundings, inhabiting the exclamation mark of their own body (or those of others they have grown used to having near them). People become their own surprises. Space and vacancy become the norm.

I started hanging out on the internet because I didn't want these things to be the norm for me—in North Dakota or anywhere else. Social media became my surrogate watercooler, a gathering place for the conversations I wasn't having in person, with the colleagues I almost never saw, since, though we worked in the same building, our working lives and schedules kept us pretty separate. Social

media populated my working days in a way that my physical surroundings could not and, thus, actually helped to make those surroundings more livable and vibrant for me. But it did not, could not,
erase the fact of my physical separation. It could only compensate.

The two poles of solitude are privilege and punishment. In America, for example, we pay for the privilege of securing access to sustained conditions of privacy—big houses with ample yards made
for keeping neighbors at a distance, or else personal vehicles that
prevent us from having to share a ride with strangers. But, at the
same time, we also wield the threat of solitude as punishment for
crimes against society. Just as we send disobedient children to their
rooms, forcing them to be alone, we sentence convicted criminals
to periods of separation from the social sphere. We demand that
they pay for their crimes via the currency of exclusion. And for
those whose crimes are judged to be particularly egregious, there
is the practice of solitary confinement, the worst of all punish-
ments that fall short of a death sentence.

We are, it seems, collectively confused about the nature and
appeal of solitude, then. Is it a good thing or a bad thing? Do we
actually desire it, or do we fear it? And if we do desire it, then what
explains our systemic reliance on it, exercised through both informal and formal means, as a method of punishment?

Of course, the difference between these two types of solitude,
between the privilege of privacy and the penalty of isolation, has to
do with choice. It is through choice that one attains, or imagines
that they are able to attain, control. To choose is to be free, to exert
power, to *win*; according to this logic, every choice is its own kind
of victory, even when it results in misery. To choose solitude, a situ-

ation that might feel like punishment if one were forced to experience it, is to exercise agency in the name of a perceived desire. Or,
another way to think of it is this: if one is alone because they choose
to be alone than they must, at heart, want to be alone.

But what if they actually don't?

What the rhetoric of freedom and choice tend to conceal in such
instances is that, when one chooses, they do not select from an infinite
array of options. Rather, they are presented with a limited set of them—
chicken or beef, say. They are made to choose from what is available,
or practical, or possible, to the point where the act of choosing starts
to look more regulated and, well, less *free*, maybe. The COVID-19 pandemic brought about a confrontation, for many, with the prospect of
solitude. Suddenly, solitude was not a choice but something that was
required—mandated, even, in certain parts of the world. Gone were
those feelings of freedom and choice. Now we were alone because we
had to be, which turned out to be a lot less fun than the kind of solitude
we had enjoyed before, back when we were allowed to decide when
and how and where we might want to experience it.

A few months ago, I was talking to a classroom full of students,
encouraging them to reflect on how the pandemic (and, in particular, a year's worth of remote college education) had affected
their social behaviors, both on- and offline. One student talked
about a growing obsession she had developed with selfies, meaning smartphone-enabled self-portraits. She explained how, a few
months into the pandemic, she had started using her phone to
take a picture of herself once a day, every day. Eventually, she had
upped the frequency of these selfies and started taking multiple
photos a day—in different situations, with different lighting, different backgrounds, etc. After a year's time, she discovered that

her phone held thousands of these pictures. So I asked her: What were you doing with them? Were you uploading them to social media? Building an Instagram presence, perhaps? She explained, though, that she wasn't interested in sharing them online. Rather, her compulsive selfie-taking had become a way, as she put it, of making sure *she was still there.*

In class, we continued to discuss this feeling she had described. It turned out, many in the room could relate to it—to the experience of being driven to test or furnish proof of one's continued physical existence. The students in the class talked about how, in a world and age that had brought about a forced reliance on virtual spaces and digital tools, their lives felt increasingly immaterial and unreal to them. Experiences felt mediated and "inauthentic," one student noted. Friendships, interactions, even educational settings had become tarnished by a creeping sense of the hollowly immaterial, by the corrosive suggestion that reality lurked elsewhere, outside of wherever a person happened to be. Students in the class talked about watching people who looked like them living out lives they couldn't quite recognize as their own. Selfies, some of them reported, were a humble means of seizing control and also of remembering what it was like to insert themselves into the stories they were watching, which were actually about them anyway.

We were talking, I realized, about out-of-body experiences. We were talking about the mind becoming so ensconced in a series of simulated environments that, despite those environments' links to physical reality, everything outside them had started to feel vague, fueling the suspicion that it might not even be there anymore. I was fascinated and stunned by the conversation. One student, for instance, reflected on the experience of celebrating Thanksgiving dinner virtually, within the confines of an online game that she was used to playing. She had a group of friends—people she had never met in person, of course—that she had come to know through the game and, because they couldn't travel to see their respective families, the group had decided they would enjoy Thanksgiving dinner together, online. She would go on to write an essay narrating the experience that included descriptions of the virtual food that the guests "ate" in each other's company. But they couldn't really eat what wasn't really there, naturally. Rather, as she explained it, they all ate real food separately and simply used the structure of the game and the virtual feast to hang out together. Mostly, that involved text conversation, plus the occasional tackling of a level or quest or mission that took place within the game itself.

Then came the ending, the point at which she finally exited the game and put her computer to sleep. The dark screen gave the image of her face back to her: suddenly, she saw herself sitting there alone in a dimly lit bedroom, on Thanksgiving. Outside, the sky had grown dark, but she hadn't noticed. She'd been playing the game and using it to hang out with her friends for almost twelve hours. The day—a holiday—was over and she hadn't even felt it passing her by. This last part, she declared, was a good thing. The game had given her shelter from a rather depressing situation. It had helped her to get through a day that offended her in feeling like any other, since the usual forms of celebration were either prohibited or impossible. She pulled up the screenshots she had taken, which showed her game avatar along with about a dozen others like it, and circulated them among the class.

There they were, the group of virtual dinner guests, seated around a virtual table, with virtual turkey drumsticks or virtual goblets of wine in their hands. They were all somewhere else, away from the bodies that they used, on other days, to move through a callous and unpredictable world. And they were all smiling.

⁓⁓⁓

Calvin Kasulke's 2021 novel *Several People Are Typing* is about a group of people who all work together in a New York City office, but who mostly do not work together in that office. Instead, the majority of them work from home, a phrase that gets reduced to an acronym, "wfh," in their staff communications. In fact, the novel takes place entirely within Slack, which is a workplace communications platform: Kasulke has the characters interact exclusively through Slack discussions, which might include the whole staff, be limited to specific project teams, or occur one-on-one through the application's direct-message feature. That means that the story in *Several People Are Typing* is limited to dialogue, and, true to the medium that contains it, that dialogue is pretty rough and casual, lacking appropriate punctuation, capitalization, and other hallmarks of formal written communication. There is no narrator, so there is no impartial voice of wisdom there to intrude upon all that dialogue, to explain it or remind the reader of what real sentences look like. There are only the scattered non sequiturs of Slack conversation, which serve to simulate the experience of one of its characters, Gerald, who finds himself trapped inside the app.

The novel opens with Gerald's discovery that his consciousness has been claimed by, or accidentally uploaded to, Slack. As a result, he can only communicate through it; his body has lost its powers of speech, along with all other physical functions except the most basic and life-sustaining ones, like breathing. Gerald's mind and body have become divorced from each other, yet each goes on "living" within its separate realm, though both require tending. His mind, for instance, searches for constant stimulation within the prison of Slack; Gerald takes to messaging his colleagues in the middle of the night because, without access to his physical body, he can't feel time passing and has forgotten what it means to sleep. Meanwhile, his body has to be cared for by a coworker who starts visiting his apartment to keeps tabs on it and assure Gerald of his continued physical existence. Those visits eventually develop into a sexual relationship with that coworker, Pradeep, who becomes attracted to Gerald's inert body even as he continues to engage with his mind separately, via Slack.

In highlighting the split between Gerald's physical and mental existence, Kasulke probes questions about what human bodies are for given what appears to be, in modern life, a situation of decreased reliance on them. If many essential human functions—like work, socialization, school, and even romance—can take place on the internet, without the active participation of the body, what becomes of the body itself? How does its role, or overall purpose, mutate given the apparent independence of the mind? At one point in the novel, for example, Gerald tries to tell Pradeep about how it feels to be separated from one's body. "it's pretty existentially terrifying," he explains, but then admits that there are certain advantages. "you know how sometimes being alive feels like this terrible cycle of eating and shitting and eating again and shitting again until you die? this is a nice break from that."[2] In losing access to his body, Gerald experiences freedom from the cyclical drudgery of bodily upkeep. He no longer feels subject to the burdens and banalities that come with physicality though, as Pradeep points out, those burdens have not been erased; they have simply been outsourced. When Pradeep later confesses his attraction to Gerald, the prospect of physical romance motivates Gerald to try to reclaim his body. That involves wresting it away from the control of the Slackbot, which is an automated platform feature that, in the novel, achieves sentience (though of a minor and dysfunctional kind) through its ongoing conversations with Gerald's captive consciousness.

Kasulke's novel brings to mind some of those conversations I was having with my students last spring. In regard to the question, *What are bodies for in a world that deprioritizes bodies?* Kasulke's book offers at least one very good answer: bodies exist for the sake of physical pleasure, including, but not limited to, sexual pleasure. In one scene, for example, Gerald tries to explain the concept of a sunset to the Slackbot. In lacking a body, a sunset is something that Gerald cannot experience or see; the same is true of the Slackbot, which, though it can be made to conceptually understand what a sunset is, lacks eyes and sensory intelligence to see it. The Slackbot responds by assembling a barrage of animated .gif files that depict various sunsets. Gerald, though, is forced to process the files as a computer would, meaning that he experiences them as lines of written code that link to, or amount to, images but cannot be "seen" in the normal, physical, human way. "it's fantastic," he tells the Slackbot, "it hurts, a little, but so does the regular sun, so."[3]

The combination of pleasure and pain that Gerald "feels," in a hypothetical sense, when he processes all of the sunset files is the closest that he, without a body, can come to experiencing what is known as the sublime. The German philosopher Immanuel Kant, who contributed to Enlightenment philosophy in theorizing connections between subjective experience and the universal appreciation of beauty, develops the idea in pieces throughout his work, including in his well-known *Critique of Judgment*, published in 1790. In it, Kant argues that there is a difference between that which is simply beautiful and that which transcends beauty and thus qualifies as sublime. The concept of beauty itself is specific to the world of objects, things that are crafted for the sake of human appreciation and judgment. What is sublime, meanwhile, exists outside of the world of human-made objects and thereby defies human understanding and aesthetic assessment; it is bigger than such things, "incommensurate with our power of exhibition, and as it were violent to our imagination, and yet we judge it all the more sublime for that," Kant writes.[4] Another way of putting it is like this: a sunset is sublime because a human cannot make one, its existence transcends human ability; meanwhile, a picture of a sunset is merely beautiful because it reflects, through human invention, a thing that no amount of human ingenuity can actually replicate in real life. What's more, a sunset is sublime because it is not made to be judged as beautiful by humans who witness it—indeed, it is not "made" with any particular purpose in mind. This is in contrast to a picture of a sunset, which is made in accordance with human appraisals of beauty. A sunset exists for no reason whereas a picture of a sunset exists to please an intended, human viewer.

Kant's focus on the sublime is but one layer to be found within a larger inquiry into human nature itself. For one of the main differences, as he sees it, between the beautiful and the sublime has to do with the ways in which humans experience each. The experience of beauty, he maintains, is an experience that points outward; appraisals of beauty are reached via external comparison and formal judgment, meaning a person's ability to see and evaluate how well a beautiful thing has been made. But the experience of the sublime points in the opposite direction, reaching inward and toward the secret contents of the self. The sublime, which is only to be found in "crude" and "magnitudinous" nature, according to Kant, displaces the human subject because that person had no hand in making it.[5] It forces them to come to terms with both the limits and possibilities of human achievement. A garden that has been tended and shaped by human hands is not sublime, but a rugged mountain landscape is because it threatens the human subject through reminders about human insufficiency. It inspires an inner search for meaning in that subject, one that arises through a confrontation with all that is not and can never be human like itself. "Hence," Kant writes, "the feeling of the sublime is a feeling of displeasure that arises from the imagination's inadequacy, in an aesthetic estimation of magnitude, for an estimation by reason, but is at the same time also a pleasure."[6]

In Kasulke's *Several People Are Typing*, Gerald arrives at an unsettling conclusion: the sublime does not and cannot exist on the internet. This is because the internet is a pure product of human manufacture. It does not come from nature; it comes, rather, from human engineering, which means that everything that exists on it—from sunset .gifs to Instagram posts to news articles to pictures of babies—is likewise made by humans. Gerald contemplates the prospect of a life lived in a world that bars him access to the sublime, a virtual world filled with

**all the people.

people stuff.

all the ephemera

the things everyone says and makes and does and manages
to post online

the daily outrages and minor amusements and short videos
and updates . . . the sublime

plopped right next to everything else[7]

Of course, the sublime "plopped right next to everything else," the
panorama of human creation, is no sublime at all, in Kant's view.
And that is the tragedy that comes from selling human existence
short, from outsourcing it to the world of virtual, as opposed to
material, confrontation. There is no sublime to be found on the
internet. That is because there is nothing but humanity to be found
on the internet.

My students, I understand, want to hang out on the internet. Most
of them would prefer it that way, because the internet offers them
some measure of control over the quality of their social interactions. It allows them to shape those experiences, to curate and
select the contents of them, and to filter out less desirable or harm-
ful ones. The process by which that is done is called *search*. It stands
opposed to a related activity, *browsing*, and summons my memories

of discussions that used to take place, led by information science scholars and librarians, about the perils of favoring one over the other. In the early 2000s, those conversations grew feverish in light of new, internet-fueled technologies that were altering the way that people accessed and read books, for instance. With the debut of the ebook, the physical codex—which refers to the form of the traditional, bound book that, unlike the scroll that came before it, can be navigated by flipping through unbound page edges—started to look antiquated. Ebooks made *keyword search* possible, which meant that a reader could use a book to look for specific phrases or information, bypassing the old process of browsing through its pages. Search, it seemed, was the signature of the new era; browsing was a thing of the past.

To search is to seek in a targeted, specific way for targeted, specific information. It's about precision, about homing in on a keyword phrase that matches, in the strictest sense possible, a chosen set of search criteria. To browse, meanwhile, involves basically the opposite. In physical terms, it amounts to trailing one's hand across the spines of books that line the shelves of a library or bookstore, waiting for something to come along that's worth pausing on and lingering over—waiting, that is, for a "happy accident" in the words of Michael Witmore, who is director of the Folger Shakespeare Library in Washington, D.C. Witmore notes that "libraries are set up to *make* such accidents happen" through what he calls "virtuous adjacency," which entails the collocation of items that are related to each other in subject matter.[8] But as another scholar on the subject, Daniel Rosenberg, points out, keyword search narrows the scope of such adjacency; it prioritizes the searcher's interaction with an algorithm, as opposed to with the human-engineered information that the algorithm has been made to retrieve or locate. "When we inter-act with search," Rosenberg argues, "we write to the computer."[9]

What's more, computer algorithms are designed to trim the fat from those user-generated keyword phrases via a process that, according to Rosenberg, is "predicated on the presumption that the important things one wished to discern from language could be established without syntax, context, or style, by accounting only for *significant words* or later *key words* and finally *keywords*."[10] Raymond Williams, again, shows how the meanings of words, even "signifi-cant" ones, can change drastically over time. Language, as Williams's work attests, is anything but stable. Keyword search, though, insists on intransigence and places much faith in stability. It is the primary mechanism that fuels contemporary use of the internet and even the algorithmic processes behind recommendations for new things to watch on Netflix and new friends to follow on Twitter, but it is marred by linguistic inflexibility and also by literalness. The result is a shallow, as opposed to deep, survey of available information and material. Life on the internet trains us for the experience of a suc-cession of surfaces, as opposed to singular depths—for the beauty of an animated sunset delivered via a .gif file, and not the sublime experience of witnessing the sunset itself as an event.

So what does it mean to hang out on the internet, when hang-ing out on the internet is necessarily backed by the comparatively shallow logic of search? It means settling for an altered quality of hanging out, one that occurs through the primary vehicle of infor-mational exchange. Text, photos, movies—they all look the same, or nearly the same, when rendered in code, which is what the char-acter Gerald realizes in *Several People Are Typing*. As a conceptual experiment, Kasulke's novel is fascinating. But it proves necessarily frustrating with regard to aesthetic enjoyment. That, of course, is the point: Kasulke is showing us, his readers, the limits of text as a social or expressive vehicle. The novel cannot express certain insights or offer much in the way of style while remaining true to the Slack chat format. This mirrors Gerald's experiences "living," or consciously residing, inside the Slack platform. There, he can communicate, but his communications can never rise above the level of data. The same is true of his impressions and experiences, which are also rendered as data. He cannot *see* the sunset; he cannot *feel* sexual attraction; he cannot *taste* the food that Pradeep feeds to his inert body in order to keep it alive. He can read about, or process data relating to, all of these things but he cannot know the meaning of any of them, not truly.

And yet many, including many of my students, would prefer to live this way. That is because there is safety and comfort to be found there in the seemingly neutral world of data, far from the riptide's threatening grasp. Bodies, after all, are messy and vulnerable; they are difficult to control and thus often subject to conquest by external forces; and they are variable, always changing on us, always defying the plans we would make and try to impose upon them. Bodies that exist in aggregate, gathered together in groups, serve to multiply those factors of vulnerability. They also feel, increasingly, like invitations to danger, as headlines about mass shootings in America continue to claim the media spotlight on an almost daily basis. Bodies can be destroyed, and modern life appears fixated on finding and broadcasting new means for their destruction.

So I understand and sympathize with my students' preference, or apparent preference, for virtual hanging out. Life, for the generation of people that I primarily teach, who are between eighteen and twenty-four years of age, has proven to be perilously unpredictable. With each new crisis that wasn't quite forecasted comes a deeper, more sincere wish for control. Where bodies can cause us to lose control, brains are touted as a mechanism for gaining and maintaining it. And, of course, there are those times when survival itself appears opposed to hanging out, where real-world dangers appear to pit the two against each other. I'm thinking of the COVID-19 pandemic, of course, which supplied us all with a fresh instance of the occasional conflict between survival and sociability. But I'm also thinking of other, historical examples, like wars.

The artist and writer Tove Jansson, for instance, was in her twenties when World War II broke out. Jansson was born in Helsinki, in what was first part of the Russian Empire and then the independent nation of Finland beginning in 1917. At the start of WWII, Finland was allied with Germany in opposition to its historical enemy, Russia, which had become the Soviet Union. That arrangement led Finland to war with the Soviets in 1941; at the same time, the German alliance created a life-threatening political situation for many Finns, including Jansson's best friend, a Russian Jewish photographer named Eva Konikoff. Jansson and Konikoff had met in the 1930s and grew close as a result of their mutual artistic passions. But in in June 1941, when Jansson was twenty-six, her best friend was forced to emigrate to the United States. Thus began long years of intense correspondence between them—of hanging out, in other words, in letters, many of which would not be received by one or the other until eight years had passed and the war had finally ended.

Jansson's letters to Eva Konikoff survive. This is in spite of the fact that Jansson—who was writing out of deep pockets of wartime despair and often to herself, since Konikoff's replies kept getting intercepted or went undelivered, just like her own—instructed her friend to burn them. The letters, though they often read like diary entries, spell out Jansson's desire to keep the conversational flame of their friendship alive. Even when she does not hear back from her friend for extended periods of time, Jansson writes and addresses her in intimate terms, refusing to concede the closeness that had developed between them. "In my studio," she writes in her first letter to Konikoff, "I found you everywhere in the things you had given me, there are so many places in town where you still walk beside me."[11] Her tone is insistent: she will not give up on her friend and will not cease being with her. She uses the medium of her correspondence as a way to keep Konikoff with her at all times, writing to her friend of minor, daily occurrences—the sort of things you might chat about via text message. This is her way of tending to the legacy of their intimacy, of keeping it watered and fresh. "I assume you haven't received any of my letters," she admits, "but I can't help writing sometimes all the same, when I'm particularly longing to have you with me again . . . I sense your presence so vividly. Everywhere I walk I remember the way it was for us in this same place a year ago."[12]

There is a magnetism to Jansson's correspondence with her friend. The momentum of her letters is riveting, as is her insistence and devotion. She will not relax her grip on her sense of optimism, or on her faith in the future. Sometimes, the act of holding on so tightly proves exhausting, as when she talks to Konikoff about having to show a brave face in the letters she sends to her lover, Tapsa, who is fighting on the front. Jansson explains how she "forced herself to write hopeful, positive, strong letters every day, when I thought the world had turned into a stinking pit."[13] What this reveals is that, in her letters, she saves her true self for her friend Eva, the only person she trusts to bear the burden of receiving it. "You don't have to understand or help me. You've nothing to do with my burden," she tells her. "But you can listen and I know you're my friend."[14]

Last spring, during one of the most difficult semesters I've yet encountered as a teacher, I was working with a group of sophomore students whose grades had landed them on academic probation. Our meetings together served the purpose of helping them to discover ways to get back on track. At one of them, I asked students in the group to name a tool, skill, or resource that might, in the coming semester, help nurture their success and work toward academic recovery. One student put it very plainly: "A friend," she said. "An in-person one." More than anything else—including time, tutoring, extended deadlines, or counseling—this student wanted, needed, a friend, someone she could see and hang out with in person. This, as she saw it, would likely have a bigger effect on her academic success than any formalized support system our college could offer her.

Reading Jansson's letters, it's clear to me that her ability to hang out with her friend Eva, even if it was forced to take place through correspondence, was key to her emotional survival during the war years. This is likewise evident given what happens after the war, when Jansson's career starts to take off (through the popularity of her whimsically illustrated Moomin books) and her correspondence with Konikoff starts to wilt. But before that happens, her letters, though more infrequent, continue to bristle with ardor and gratitude. In a letter dating from 1946, after the war has ended, she writes, "Thanks, loyal friend, for providing so many golden moments these past few years!"[15] The moments that Jansson speaks of have been achieved through correspondence and the occasional parcel sent through the mail; she is still years away from being physically reunited with her friend. Yet those moments, little pieces of time in which her friend has been made amorphously present to her, have been a lifeline—a charged connection that succeeded in reaching beyond the borders of Jansson's solitude and isolation in Helsinki. She never stops being grateful for her friend's attention, even when she cannot receive clear proof of it in the form of written responses. And she never stops being grateful, in a more ironic sense, for the distance that lies between herself and her friend, which is the only thing that has kept Konikoff safe. She frequently refers to the fact of that distance in her letters, styling it as a boon that, while it has made their hanging out more difficult, has also made its continuation possible.

There is a lot to learn about what hanging out on the internet can be from the history of what hanging out via correspondence has *had* to be, in light of dangerous circumstances. Hanging out on the internet, it must be said, is safe—or safer, at any rate, when viewed in light of the countless material hazards that continue to plague our modern world. But in prioritizing that sense of safety, we run the risk of misconstruing the relationship between it and hanging out. That connection is not automatic or inevitable; sometimes, it might not even be preferable.

To seek the sublime, for instance, is a dangerous undertaking. It involves facing up to what is itself unknown and unfamiliar. That is why it can't be done from home, or from the safety of one's phone or computer. That which is deemed sublime, according to Kant, stages a confrontation between inward fear and outward mastery. But just as the starving person does not have the luxury of taste and so cannot pause to choose whichever foods are most delicious or nourishing, so the fearful person cannot comprehend the sublime, which inspires fear but also a concomitant belief in mastery and might. When you climb a tall mountain, for instance, you're likely to experience a number of obstacles along the way: physical exhaustion, punishing weather and resulting bodily discomfort, hunger, thirst, and perhaps a fair amount of pain. But when you get to the top, you are faced with an incredible vista—snow-capped peaks spreading into the blue of distance—that talks back and tells you the story of what you have just done and all that you have accomplished. It shows you, in other words, where physical discomfort has gotten you. "That is why the agreeableness that arises from the cessation of a hardship is *gladness*," Kant writes, commenting on the way that euphoria often follows upon an experience of discomfort. And that is why, he argues, "we like to call these objects sublime because they raise the soul's fortitude above its usual middle range and allow us to discover in ourselves an ability to resist . . . [to believe] that we could be a match for nature's seeming omnipotence."[16]

To seek the sublime is to practice resistance, to pilgrimage and meet resistance where it is, to embark on an experimental kind of encounter with it. And that, crucially, is not something that can happen online, within the human-engineered space of the internet, which, in reality, is no space at all. I am not advocating for hanging out in pointedly dangerous circumstances. I do not view such circumstances as the necessary inverse of what it means to hang out online (the internet, after all, has its own dangers). But I am arguing for a practical exploration of what danger means and where it can be found, two things that are likely to look a little bit different to each individual explorer. To seek the sublime, an act that is fundamental to true human experience, according to Kant, involves a journey beyond the point of comfort. It demands a thorough investigation of the terrain that lies beyond everything that already feels familiar. And, sometimes, it requires getting to that point and simply turning around again. The journey back toward the familiar can be intelligently plotted if one makes it while armed with a new awareness of unfamiliarity.

Once, several years ago, I was descending a mountain in the company of my father and a few of his friends, and we fell, the whole group of us. There were four of us tied into the line there on Mt. Three Fingers, which is in Washington state, and my dad, who was in the lead, started to slip. It was August and we were traversing the top edge of the Queest-alb Glacier, as it is known, and working our way across its slick, sun-warmed face. I saw it happen, saw my dad fumble for the ice axe that was strapped to his wrist, saw him scramble to turn over and put its blade in, saw his sunglasses go skittering down the mountain. I watched it all with frozen dread, knowing that I would be pulled off, that I would be the next to fall. I didn't scream, there was no time. I made a quick attempt to get the tip of my ice axe into the lip of the glacier. And then I waited. It didn't take long. The axe didn't hold, having been inserted too hastily and in a place where the ice was too thin. In an instant, the snow beneath my feet turned to air.

Out of the four of us on the line, two managed to self-arrest and get their ice axes to do exactly what we had intended them to do when we dragged them with us all the way up the mountain. But I was not one of them. I dangled there in the wind between numbers two and four—between Andy, a character who you might remember from the previous chapter, and his father, Bill. At eighty-four years old, Bill was our anchor, not because he was the strongest but because he had the most experience. And it was a good thing too. Because I, sixty years his junior, was busy staring into the open throat of my worst nightmares, swinging in the breeze, and heaving. The rope that Bill was anchoring had caught me tight around my rib cage and caused me to vomit. For a moment, I simply hung there and watched the orange puddle of my innards slide down the glacier. Then I got my act together, with the help of the others, including my dad, who was already using his axe to climb back up to Andy and Bill's level, some thirty or fifty feet above us. I started to follow him, using my feet to cut steps into the wall of ice as I went. It was slow going and my breath was still squeezed by fear and not coming like it should. But I got back up. We all did. Then we proceeded carefully to the other side of the glacier, to a resting spot on a rocky ridge that mountaineering guides call either Tin Can Gap or Tin Pan Gap.

We sat there for a while, with the sun on our backs and the high, cold wind swirling around us. Nobody spoke until, at length, Bill broke the silence, saying, "Yes, I think this might be the last time I come up here." In the moment, I was ready to agree with him. But since then, years of living have softened my outlook on the memory of nearly dying. It must be the same for my dad because he has returned to the summit of Mt. Three Fingers, which was always one of his favorites, several times. In fact, he was just there last summer, at the age of seventy. And though I have not been back myself, I continue to seek out places like it, meaning places that scare me. These are the places, by the way, that give rise to stories—that send little hits of the sublime coursing through one's bloodstream. To hang out in such places is to contribute to the making of a special kind of true story, one that exceeds the constraints of genre and data by insisting on sensation and experience. To hang out in such places in the company of others is to set the stage for the collective telling of such a story.

Is contact with the sublime necessary, then? Does it have to happen in order for a person to be a person, or to live the type of life that it is our unique privilege, as humans, to choose to live? What I'm saying, what I'm arguing, what I've been contending all throughout this book, is *yes*. But the good news is that the sublime can be found in many places. If the search for it is really about the search for resistance—about discovering those spots where forward momentum founders and things get difficult, or the story swerves and heads into uncharted or less-charted territory—then it stands to reason that it can be found in many places and under many circumstances. It just can't be found at home. It lies elsewhere, beyond the perimeters of human construction, out there with the meteor showers and the glaciers and the sunsets. So does the feeling. So does the euphoria.

CONCLUSION

HOW TO

HANG OUT

A few months ago, I was in a bar in Milwaukee with a friend, and we had a fight.

Not a big fight, mind you, but a disagreement, one that felt important enough to set hackles quivering on both sides. I've known this friend for a long time, since college; indeed, if that weren't the case, the fight probably wouldn't have happened in the first place, since reasoned disagreement rests on the kind of trust that only comes with familiarity. At any rate, we were in this bar, drinking what one drinks in Milwaukee, by which I mean brandy old-fashioneds. It was a low-lit, divey sort of place located near the hotel where I was staying. I was in town to attend a series of organizational meetings and my friend Ronny had come up on the train from Chicago to spend the evening with me. We had had dinner together and then retreated to the bar in question, where red velvet curtains divided shadowy booths and the music was low enough to allow for conversation. And then we had this fight.

The details of it don't matter anymore. What matters is that my friend and I stayed in that bar for three hours, talking and digesting the disagreement that had sprung up between us, until it ceased to be a disagreement at all. In talking it out, we realized that we were actually on the same side; we wanted a lot of the same things, we just had different ideas about how to achieve them. When it was over, we found ourselves somewhere new, having emerged from the clouds that had gathered over our debate but were always destined to dispel if given enough time.

We left the bar as we had entered it hours before—as old friends, except by then it felt like the fiber of our relationship had grown tougher somehow, like it had been productively tested. That toughening, I believe, comes as the unique result of care. My friend and I care about each other, enough to not give up and not stay mad. Nobody stormed out or left the table, though the compulsion to do so may well have presented itself at some point. Instead, we both stuck it out, ascending to what felt like the precipice of personal offense and anger and then, together, descending a trail we had found leading down the other side.

From this experience, I got to thinking about how friendship and hanging out alike require stamina. Sometimes, we have to let things be long and loose in order for them to pass through a crucial point of conflict and then get good again. The problem, though, comes from how the pace of modern living conditions us for the opposite, for rapid-fire experiences and instantaneous judgments. Enthusiasm and ardor get kindled quickly, but so do dislike and dismissal. As a result, we make a habit of turning away from all the things and people and encounters that bother, confuse, or tax us. We abandon them, comforting ourselves with excuses about how they're not worth our time anyway. We swivel our attention elsewhere, settling our sights on new, temporary targets. And then, seconds or minutes later, we go and do it all again.

These are habits gleaned from constant and repeated exposure to a stimulant-rich mediaverse, what Jenny Odell and others, including the French thinker Yves Citton, call "the attention economy." That mediaverse teaches us to fear for our attentional capacities because it views them as anchored in a set of finite resources. As Citton explains it, "While the calculations of the classical economy of material goods are based on the scarcity of factors of *production*, the attention economy is based on the scarcity of the capacity for the *reception* of cultural goods."[1] Citton is talking about the way that culture, as a system of commodified production, works by capturing the attention of receptive audiences. But the same point, I think, is true where society and social experiences are concerned. There is not enough time, we are told, to just thoughtlessly give our time away, to waste it on things and people who are of dubious value. But what held my friend and me there in that velvet-draped booth at that bar in Milwaukee, through all the uncomfortable twists of our heated disagreement, was, I want to argue, the exact opposite: it was a kind of faith in time itself. We were there to spend the evening together and so had already decided to dedicate that time to each other. As a result, we did not feel threatened by the specter of a premature conclusion.

But let's imagine, for the sake of contrast, that this fight of ours had happened under different circumstances—online, say, or even via text message. Would we have had the stamina to stick it out and wait for things to resolve? Or would we have turned our attention away from each other at the first sign of conflict, seeking refuge in a new tab, a new search result, a new notification, a new follower, a new timeline refresh? Would we have listened to each other and made an effort to understand? Or would we have exited the tab, closed the screen, muted, or even blocked each other, out of frustration? Would we have believed, without looking the other person in the eye, in the prospect of our conflict's eventual resolution? Or would we have allowed spirals of miscommunication, anxiety, and self-doubt to lead us straight to the point of a silent impasse?

What I'm trying to show by way of this conjecture is that, while modern communications technologies tend to make the space of even friendly disagreement feel more narrow and thus also more uncomfortable, hanging out is actually about the opposite. Hanging out, which involves killing time in the presence of others, is about carving out a space that is big enough to accommodate these kinds of relational fluctuations, allowing them to stretch and unfurl as necessary. It's a way of announcing up front that it doesn't always have to be good, that we don't always have to catch a person on a good day in order to care about or honor our connection to them. Hanging out means marking out a space that is big enough to house both the camaraderie that gets built in the moment along with mistakes, attitudinal spikes, and second chances.

So what does it mean to hang out now, and how does one do it?

Writing this book has been, for me, like a sojourn into a poorly mapped territory. The terrain is hard to pick out from the squiggly lines and shapes that appear drawn on that map; all I know for sure is that the region is bordered on either side by these two questions, by *what* and *how*. At times I have felt myself drifting toward one side or the other, lured by puzzles about meaning and then also by proscriptive inclinations. And, all the while, I have had to keep interrogating my status as an authority, wondering if I have any right to set down rules for myself—let alone others—about how hanging out ought to happen or work. After all, I don't pretend to be an expert on the subject, nor do I pretend that expertise is even possible where the subject is concerned. A person does not excel or fail at hanging out so much as they do it or they don't.

But in talking to friends, colleagues, acquaintances, and family members about this book, and about the concept of hanging out, I've become an accidental witness to a growing crisis. It's a quiet catastrophe, one that has been building steam for some time, and it's an unmistakably toxic one. I've noticed people struggling to hang out, or else voicing concern and anxiety about how to hang out. I've also seen these people, my own friends, wrestling with panic and fear where hanging out is concerned, overthinking certain procedural moves, dwelling on unintended fallout and, at times, scarred by all the effort and personal sacrifice that it has cost them. All of this has led me to conclude that, where hanging out and casual social interaction are concerned, we have reached a collective tipping point. Though perhaps not the original cause of this crisis, the pandemic was the catalyst that helped transfer the majority of our social energies to the internet, as I argued back in the Introduction. What this means is that we have already come up and over the high mountain ridge that divides the old world of analog social reality from the new one. We have two choices, then, and only one of them is real: retreat, or learn how to live here in this new country.

Recently, I was talking to an old friend of mine, E.M., who mentioned that they were struggling to make friends in this new country. E.M. is queer, identifying as nonbinary transmasculine, and also the parent of a toddler. This situation keeps them mostly home-bound and makes accessing certain traditional queer spaces, like bars and clubs, extra difficult for them. They explained that they had started experimenting with the use of an app called Lex in order to meet friends. According to its website, Lex exists to connect "queer lovers and friends" through the medium of text-based exchanges.[2] This distinguishes it from popular queer networking apps like Grindr, which encourage users to appraise each other through visuals alone, incentivizing that style of instantaneous judgment that I mentioned before. I asked E.M. to send me their profile write-up, so I could see how they were presenting and, well, *marketing* themselves for potential friendships via Lex. Because that's what I saw happening: friendship requires time and, in a world where time is judged to be in short supply, time-consuming ventures like friendship become subject to the pressures of market-style logic. Competition then ensues, as a means of weeding out unworthy elements and guiding the consumer toward the safest investment or choice. Marketing tactics are then used to persuade the customer into thinking that one choice is better, or more appropriate for them, than another.

One particular phrase from my friend's profile, or self-marketing plan, stood out to me: "extroversion-curious." I have known my friend E.M. for about twenty years and I have never known them to be shy. In fact, when I think back to when I first met them in college, I recall the role that they played as a social leader on our campus, serving as editor in chief of our school newspaper, bringing musical acts to our campus and overseeing their shows in our student union, living in a co-op house where everyone volunteered on behalf of a local environmental organization, throwing parties, organizing vegan dinners—the list goes on. Could these, I wondered, be the actions of an introvert with "extroversion-curious" leanings? Or had things changed for my friend in the past decades, and thus *changed my friend*? And if so, how did that happen?

It's no secret that modern life is isolating and that, if anything, it looks to be headed in the direction of increased, not decreased, isolation. In talking to my friend E.M., I kept thinking about all that had transpired since our college days to cement those conditions of isolation to the point where we all started to see them as not just normal but ineluctable. That word, *ineluctable*, by the way, contains the Latin verb *luctor*, which means "to struggle." When combined with the prefix *e-*, which means "out" (as in *egress*), the verb means "to struggle out of something." And finally, when we add on the additional prefix *in-*, which means "not" (as in *inverse*), we get this: the inability to struggle out of something, or an adjective describing something from which someone cannot wriggle free. We get a straitjacket, in other words—a devastatingly appropriate way of describing our current situation with regard to social activity and hanging out.

So while I want to resist the rhetoric of rules and guidelines here, I also want to help fill in the blank spaces along that sketchily drawn map. I want, in other words, to throw up a few signposts for the sake of fellow travelers (like my friend E.M. and, I suspect, like many others too). This means insisting on a set of what are not quite rules but more like reminders, since they are drawn from communal social logic and also from a historical understanding of what we, as humans, have a long history of exceling at. It's a bit like when my yoga teacher issues reminders about a pose I have held hundreds of times before: the goal is not to admonish or point out how and where I'm doing it wrong, but to prompt me to remember what I already know about how to do it better, to tap into that buried knowledge and haul it back out into the light so that it can rest there on the surface of my awareness.

The rules are simple, and they're not really rules. Rather, I want to think of them as cues to spur a kind of thinking that we already have access to but, it seems, could stand to become reacquainted with. They're grammatically styled as commands here because each one involves the intentional seizure of something. The command form is there to serve as a gentle reminder that these cues are not invitations for passive reflection but, in fact, calls to action. Together, they encourage active participation in a whole choreography of devotion—of care-informed capture, if you will.

They go like this:

1. TAKE TIME.

This is the most important one because it's where it all starts. Hanging out cannot happen without time—that is, without the strategic confiscation of it.

We must wrest time away from the places where it has been sequestered and kept from us against our will. We must work to seize and redistribute the wealth that is time and, when we have done that, we must commit to the work of giving it all back to each other. This means taking the time to listen. It means letting others talk. It means taking the time, even, to notice when there is nothing to listen to or talk about, to discover the companionable qualities of stillness and silence. And, perhaps most significantly, it means taking the time to let things pass from good to bad to good again, to see the whole thing through beyond the point of discomfort, which is often a part of hanging out but usually temporary anyway.

Back in that bar in Milwaukee, my friend could have walked out on me. He even joked about doing it, at one point, asking if he needed to find another place to sleep, since we were supposed to be sharing a hotel room. But though his body was already visibly tense with frustration, he did not use it to get up and flee. We stayed there together, locked into that moment of discomfort and jointly committed to transforming it into something else—something other than an ending. We took time and we also gave it, to each other. But all of that started with the act of claiming it in the first place.

Taking time means just that—taking, seizing, capturing—but it also requires the vigilant protection of what little time is already there. While our employers preach to us about the perils of "time theft" (a former employer of mine did this, subjecting us workers to computerized training modules that quizzed us about appropriate uses of company time), many of us perform jobs that cannot be done in forty hours a week, or in whatever amount of time has been allotted for our contractual working of them. As a result, we leave work each day with the feeling that we are turning our backs on heaps of unfinished business, on a mass of toil and terror that is only likely to fester and grow while we're not looking. So we do what we can during our nonworking hours to make it all more bearable, to hack away at the mountain of what must be done. We send emails. We text. We check the group chat. We squeeze in a couple of extra minutes, hours, whatever we can filch from our own personal stores of time.

This is how our work becomes, in the words of *Atlantic* writer Derek Thompson, "an archipelago of productivity amid a sea of chores, meals, mental breaks, and other responsibilities." Thompson writes of the third "peak," or spike, in productivity experienced by modern workers, especially in the wake of the COVID-19 pandemic, which has trampled on what were already blurry lines separating work from nonwork. It was Microsoft that first diagnosed this third peak by tracking their workers' "keyboard events," meaning their use of strictly work-related computer applications. The pandemic, they concluded, had resulted in a more dispersed workday, in part because more people were working from home and so unable to physically flee their own working environments. But along with that dispersal came, simply, more work. "The average workday has expanded by 13 percent—about an hour—since March 2020, and average after-hours work has increased by twice as much," Thompson reports, synthesizing findings from the Microsoft study.[3]

This compares to the observations of Theodor Adorno. Writing in the 1940s and '50s, Adorno observed how the phrase "free time" was used to conceal what was, in truth, a pernicious extension of working time. "Free time is shackled to its opposite," Adorno points out, and then goes on to question the fate of an experience that is, using that metaphor of forced physical attachment, "shackled to" everything it's not supposed to be. Adorno asks, "what becomes of free time, where productivity of labour continues to rise, under persisting conditions of unfreedom . . . ?" The answer, he concludes, is that free time becomes a "parody of itself"—*unfree* in every sense except its name, since it both costs money and is meant to restore the worker's productive faculties and render them fit for working again.[4] What this means is that free time, when there is not enough of it to go around, is primarily experienced as *work-preparation* time, since the benefits of leisure are then reaped through the worker's eventual return to work. This is why Adorno, in his essay "Free Time," critiques the activities that nominally pass for "leisure" in American culture. He looks askance at pursuits like camping, going to the cinema, and watching television, not because they are inherently bad but because they serve the primary purpose of reinvigorating the poor, doomed worker. This recalls Mark Greif's arguments, about how reality television is not enjoyable in itself but, rather, an efficient means of tricking the viewer into believing that joy can be derived from watching others experience it. Television, especially reality television, lets us eavesdrop on others' efforts to hang out and experience leisure.

Today, time is being stolen *from us*—not for the first time, as Adorno would be quick to point out, but at newly unprecedented rates. After all, it's not like we workers are getting richer by doing all that extra work outside of our normally contracted working hours (indeed, we are not, thanks to forty years of wage suppression, a term that refers to the way that wages for laborers are kept low and allowed to stagnate while high-ranking corporate owners and managers receive ever bigger payouts, bonuses, and salaries). In order to safeguard what little time we have, and while we are working on stealing the rest back, we must develop an awareness of the boundaries that exist to protect it. We have to fortify those boundaries and help to make them more visible and substantial, able to withstand new forms of attack.

Recently, I was corresponding with a colleague in France, where a full-time workweek is capped at thirty-five hours and workers can claim the right to abstain from sending or receiving emails on the weekend. My colleague and I were working on a joint grant application that had to be filed the following week. "Would you be comfortable receiving an email on a Saturday?" she asked me.

I was floored. No one had ever asked me such a question before.

Indeed, when I met my friend Ronny in that bar in Milwaukee, I was there because I was working on a Saturday, for free. Worse than that, I was paying to do it, having bought my own airfare (the hotel was comped, at least). So why was I there, working on a week-end? Who had required me to be there?

The answer is: me. At an earlier age and an earlier stage of my career, I said yes to everything, because I feared I lacked the power to say anything else. I dug a deep hole for myself and lined it with the word *yes*. I didn't realize that *yes* was the first step down a road of professional commitments that would spread out to blanket whole years of my life. I didn't believe in my own right to boundar-ies, didn't believe I deserved them.

But I do. *We all do.* This is why hanging out begins with taking time, looting and liberating it from the coercions of fear and com-plicity. We must take time in order to kill it and render its defenses against us inert. We must take time in order to understand what it means to have it, which is the first step to dreaming about what else we might do with it.

2. TAKE RISKS.

Earlier in this book, I wrote about hanging out with strangers—a risky undertaking, if we are to believe examples provided by films like *Victoria*. But most of the risks that we take when we meet some-one new or chat with a stranger are pretty minimal and they come at little cost to us. This is wisdom that I have been forced to learn, I will admit, through a series of accidents in itinerant living. I have lived in a lot of places, not because I planned to but because educa-tion, jobs, opportunities, and relationships compelled me to. As a result, I sometimes feel that I am more acquainted with the experi-ence of being a stranger—of feeling my way through new acquain-tances, cultural codes, and regional niceties—than I am with that of being a local, an insider, whatever you want to call it. And I'm okay with this. As much I believe in Odell's notion of "placefulness" and getting to know a place as best one can, through "sensitivity and responsibility to the historical (what happened here) and the ecological (who or what lives, or lived, here),"[5] I also find that being a stranger has certain advantages. For one, it keeps the essential faculties of awareness, which are required to both study the historical and observe the ecological, sharp and running at full steam. The stranger does not get to claim the privileges of nativist knowledge, but neither are they as susceptible to the fog of familiarity that, sometimes, comes with those privileges. The stranger has to remain alert and vigilant, taking in cues and learning new ways for being in the world. Maintaining that level of alertness can be exhausting, yes, but it is not without its own rewards.

For example, during the first year that I was living in Vermont, I found that I was barred from accessing most regular opportunities for hanging out. I was a stranger and looking to meet new people, but I couldn't go out and frequent the kinds of spaces where people hung out. Bars, restaurants, libraries, coffee shops, gyms, yoga studios, and even the campus where I worked, they were all closed. But the mountains weren't. My partner and I hiked twenty-one mountains in about eleven months. On top of one them, Belvidere Mountain, we stopped to catch our breath, scale the rickety old fire tower for views of the surrounding valleys, and have some lunch. It was a cold and gray day, one that teetered on the edge of seasons, with spring starting to spread along the valley floor while the winds of winter held strong up top. Another couple had gotten to the summit before us and the four of us got to talking about how we'd managed the last half mile or so of snow, comparing gear and boots.

This turned into an exchange of phone numbers and a proposal to meet up and hike together. After a while, those outings segued into dinner gatherings and other forms of hanging out. Now we count these people as friends. (None of this would have happened, by the way, if my partner and I had been wearing earbuds or headphones at the time, something that I see a lot of hikers doing these days. So while we're speaking of taking risks, consider *taking your headphones off* now and then, too, and exposing yourself to the potential of your real-world sonic environment.)

The risk in this case was minimal. Sometimes, I know, it can feel like a lot more. Because what we worry about risking, or losing, when we take chances on strangers is a sense of ease and also the safety of our own comfort. We risk bringing discomfort upon ourselves when we enter into situations that lack foreseeable parameters or outcomes. We also risk rejection, which, at bottom, is really about personal discomfiture. But insofar as discomfort is linked to its inverse, to comfort—because we cannot know and define one sensation without having some experience of the other—hanging out can be a way to keep the two in balance, to force a person to constantly confront and reckon with the definitions of each. What this means is that hanging out, sometimes, needs to be a little bit risky and a little bit uncomfortable too.

But not a lot uncomfortable. There ought to be limits, after all, and a commonsense awareness of red flags. We do not, any of us, need to suffer bullies or braggarts or manipulative jerks in the name of hanging out. But we do need, I think, to remember to see the value in situations that challenge or test us, so long as those tests can occur within supportive settings. This, by the way, is precisely what education is all about, which is something that I often try to explain to my own students. Educational settings, like classrooms, offer low-risk opportunities for experimentation and for the application of skills that require testing in order to reach full maturation. In the kind of classroom I tend to hang around, by which I mean the writing classroom, this means writing for an audience of what Octavia E. Butler calls "rented readers"[6]—an audience that can be purchased, for example, via tuition payments. If hanging out is about improvisation, as I have argued elsewhere in this book, then that means locating the types of people and environments that are able, willing, and interested in playing host to that improvisation.

It also means avoiding those who would use the excuse of standards or traditions or rules to intimidate and guard their gates against new entrants. Hanging out can be about bravery, but it shouldn't have to *always* be about bravery.

3. TAKE—AND CREATE—OPPORTUNITIES.

My parents celebrated their fiftieth wedding anniversary in December of 2020, while the pandemic was still raging and before vaccines had tempered its progress, even. My sister and I had, years before, mused on the prospect of throwing a party for them to mark the occasion. But those plans withered quite predictably in the face of worldwide lockdowns. Instead, my parents celebrated with a party for two. They went to their favorite restaurant, located on Seattle's Lake Union—a place where, before the pandemic, the bartenders and servers knew their names and my mom didn't even have to order her favorite lime-basil-gin cocktail because, the second they saw her coming through the door, they would start getting it ready. For their anniversary party of two, though, there were no servers on hand: the restaurant, like all restaurants, had been relegated to takeout-only orders for some months. So they drove to Lake Union, ordered a couple of their favorite items to-go, picked them up, and ate them in the parking lot inside my dad's van. They brought a bottle of champagne to go with their clam chowder because the restaurant had cut back on bar service and they couldn't get my mom's usual cocktail. My dad texted me a photo, a selfie he'd taken of the two of them seated there in the back of the van, plastic cups of champagne raised toward the camera.

I know the occasion wasn't an ideal one for them, but it was something—an attempt, a venture, an effort. I felt happy and proud of them for making it so even as I regretted not being there, regretted my powerlessness and inability to make it something more for them. This is part, I think, of the bundle of lessons that has been inelegantly dropped upon us by the pandemic, though the insight itself is not necessarily a new one. In having to forgo a preprogrammed array of celebrations and events and get-togethers, we have been forced—given a unique chance, one might also say—to reconsider the meaning and purpose of such rituals. Periodic celebrations provide a way of marking time, of course. But I think that observances of this kind are significant not simply for what they reinforce, in terms of routine, but for how they break and bend the rhythms of routine, injecting spaces between the notes that, maybe, help us to pick out the melody of life a bit more clearly. This idea recalls a line from Virginia Woolf's *To the Lighthouse*, which is basically a novel about a dinner party: "The great revelation had never come. The great revelations perhaps never did come. Instead there were little daily miracles, illuminations, matches struck unexpectedly in the dark."[7]

I like to think that my parents' fiftieth anniversary celebration, as humble as it was, was one of those moments of quiet illumination born from the mere strike of a metaphorical match. I hope that its spark helped to hollow out a space in the dark for them, as it did for me when I saw the picture and thought about them there, eating clam chowder in the back of the van while the sun set down behind Queen Anne Hill and all the little colored lights of the city came out hotter and stronger.

Often, it is our approach to the prospect of hanging out that proves to be the source of trouble and likewise discomfort. We pile expectations upon little things, instances, and events that are not large enough or strong enough to hold the weight of all that we would ask of them. This is the lesson that Mick Kelly learns in Carson McCullers's *The Heart Is a Lonely Hunter*. Mick discovers that she has asked too much of both herself and of the party that she wanted to throw, the one that was supposed to transform her into two things: an adult and a more cultured, elite person. Mick is her own enemy in this scenario and also the only one preventing her from having a good time at the *real* party, the one that ensues.

Mick's experiences show us that if we can keep humility and practicality in sight when hanging out, then we just might be able to have a good time doing it. I'm thinking of my childhood best friend, Marta, who, these days, is a busy mother to two young boys. Because we live on opposite coasts, I only get to see her about once a year and so, when I do, I try to let it happen under her terms. I don't care if that means running errands with her, or sitting by her side in a doctor's waiting room because one kid has an earache. The goal, for me, is simply to settle in and occupy whatever opportunities may present themselves. This requires making myself as flexible as possible and, to the best of my ability, muting any and all expectations. I find that if I do this, then I am rewarded with an opportunity of the rarest kind: the chance to see my friend exactly as she is now, her world, and her life, which is the truest form of intimacy I can conceive of.

4. TAKE CARE.

This involves the conscious and repeated extension of care to oneself and to others. I'm not talking about "self-care," one of corporate America's favorite pet phrases, designed to shift the burden of care away from those who possess the most power to furnish it and, instead, heap it onto the shoulders of the already-suffering individual who, on top of all that suffering, is then coerced into making up for the shortfall of care that was the original cause of their torment. No, I'm not talking about that; I'm talking about care as a radical form of investment and risk. To care requires making a sincere effort. Care is the soil from which all actions that actually matter have to grow, because the opposite, disinterest, is barren ground.

The problem is that care, much like attention and time, is in short supply. Or that's what the contemporary mediaverse, whose job it is to manufacture new fresh hells for us to care about, would have us believe. Adorno's specific term for that mediaverse, the one that he and Max Horkheimer coined back in the late 1940s, is "the culture industry." He uses this term to describe a system of mass distraction, a superficial "parade [of] progress" that touts the "incessantly new," but which is actually structured by a dependence on sameness, standardization, and the dispensing of familiarity.

"Everywhere the changes mask a skeleton which has changed just as little as the profit motive itself," Adorno writes.[8] If the culture industry's job, starting in the post-war era, was to keep everyone distracted, than the contemporary mediaverse's job combines that function with another, added one: draining us of our capacity for care. Distracted people make for bad political agents and citizens. But even worse than a distracted citizenry is one that has become disinterested and *stopped* caring. To cease to care is to cease to live in the company of ethical questions and also of each other.

This is why hanging out must be made to rest on a pledge of care. When looking away, dropping out, and changing the channel are all incentivized, then care itself becomes a radical concept. We must cultivate care but we must do so, well, *carefully*, with an awareness of the conditions that it needs to thrive and also of the dangers that threaten and surround it. That means taking care of ourselves and, when necessary, releasing ourselves from our commitments to situations that feel, at best, like one-way streets and, at worse, like dead ends or cul-de-sacs—places where care gets deposited without flowing back into and nourishing the general fund of human feeling. What I'm talking about are those situations where, after repeated trials or tests, we find that our care is not rewarded, honored, or matched. I believe in second chances; I believe that hanging out involves creating arenas for the staging of second chances, for acts of redemption; but I also believe that, inside such arenas, a person has to keep a mental inventory of all the exits. And when pressed to do so, they have to summon the courage to use them.

A good example of this is the book *Trainspotting*, which I discussed previously with regard to hanging out with strangers. In

being a book about addiction, and drug addiction in particular, *Trainspotting* is about the struggle to stop hanging out as
much as it is a survey of a particular social architecture associated with hanging out. The main character in it, Mark Renton,
grasps the need to make changes to his life. Indeed, that is why
he is the main character, because his psychology is roomy and
detailed enough to allow for that classic character "arc," as we
writers and writing teachers like to call it. Such an arc has to
be achieved through growth and change. Mark changes while
the others around him do not, or cannot, or else refuse to. That
makes him different and also, ironically, puts him in the position
of having to make antisocial choices. He grows away from his old
friends but also becomes a healthier person, one who may well
prove more capable of locating and securing healthier friendships down the line.

Taking care, then, is really about taking stock. For instance, I
talk a lot about alcohol in this book, because alcohol is, for many, a
substance that facilitates hanging out. But a lot of my friends these
days are recovering alcoholics, or parents to breastfeeding children,
or people who have chosen to give up alcohol for health reasons.
Because I refuse to leave them out, and because I want to honor the
changes that they have made in the name of caring for themselves,
my own approach to hanging out has adjusted to account for these
variations. And what I've found is that it can be easily done: these
changes can be easily made and painlessly incorporated, especially
when they are carried out under the umbrella of care. As my friend
Émile once learned from his quest for the long lost bottle of wine,
it's never really about the wine anyway.

5. TAKE HEART.

This is perhaps both the simplest and the most complex of all the cues I propose here. It amounts to the cultivation of resilience, a word that I generally detest because, like "self-care," it often comes coupled with expectations about enduring or rebounding from abuse. But resilience is not only a core part of hanging out; it's a means for survival. We have to survive what harms and hurts bolstered by the knowledge that it doesn't always have to be that way, that it won't always be that way.

Taking heart, then, is about cultivating that M.F.K. Fisher–like faith in the future: there will be butter, there will be eggs, and there will be dinner parties made from butter and eggs, or their equivalents, even if we find ourselves lacking all of these things right now. What is bad can, in fact, get better; this is the mantra that lies at the heart of any inclinations toward progress. It's a way of fastening our gazes to the horizon, of telling ourselves that what feels hard today may well start to feel easy tomorrow. The key lies in both practice and in the adoption of a generous, flexible outlook. Hanging out requires the repeated exertion and application of one's social capacities. That can feel exhausting, sure—in the same way, maybe, that the thought of attending a party that starts at 11:00 p.m. (like the "non-Facebook" parties I used to go to) feels mildly exhausting to me now. But as with all things, the first attempt is the hardest and after that, momentum can be counted on to bear an increasing proportion of the weight of whatever follows.

When that momentum peters out and fades, or gets cut short, then that is the time to really and truly take heart. That is when it becomes necessary to gather up the energy that has resulted from all that previous action, to cradle it gently in your hands and commit to replanting it elsewhere, in new and unfamiliar ground. It's tricky, but it can be done; I've seen it; I've done it.

In North Dakota, for instance, two of my most beloved colleagues were Sherry and Virgil, the couple who I mentioned back in the Introduction to this book. They taught my partner, Dave, and me not just about the institutional realities that governed our working lives there but also about the history and culture of the plains, about resilience and all the many rewards of care, and about farming. Each spring, Virgil would show up at our house, unannounced and unbidden, to drop off a truck bed full of aged manure that came courtesy of his flock of sheep. The manure, he promised, would enhance my own efforts at what I varyingly called light farming or heavy gardening. Sherry and Virgil, in addition to being college professors, were veterans of the plains; they knew how everything grew there and their charity and generosity toward the place felt as limitless as the landscape. They helped launch nonprofit organizations and charitable projects dedicated to the preservation of various branches of local knowledge—traditional Métis culture, fiber arts and the sustainable animal husbandry needed to support it, and responsible stewardship of the land. Our final goodbyes in North Dakota were to them, but they weren't sad: Sherry and Virgil were too busy loading up our car with farm-fresh provisions for the trip, which included cucumbers and squashes and raspberries packed into coolers and bottles of box elder maple syrup. Sadness wielded too dull a blade to cut through the frenzy of what was to be our last chance at hanging out.

When I landed in Vermont, I was looking to transfer some of the energy that had been kindled through my interactions with Sherry and Virgil, and others like them, back in North Dakota. I started volunteering at the Intervale Community Farm, which is located on a historic floodplain right in the middle of the city of Burlington, on a piece of land that was once deemed blighted and unusable. Under the direction of a sprightly volunteer coordinator named Bonnie, in whom I saw quite a lot of my old friends Sherry and Virgil, I became part of a group that meets regularly to weed, cull, trim, prune, and, well, hang out, in a productive and hands-on sense. The first time, I will admit, it was a little hard; I arrived at the farm along with the rising sun and then worked for six straight hours chopping down box elder trees. As I did, I started talking to Bonnie and some of the other volunteers: "Did you know syrup can be made from box elder, just like with other varieties of maple?"

Bonnie was stunned: she had no idea. I started telling her about my friends Sherry and Virgil and about the syrup they had made from the trees that lined the borders of their farm back in Minnesota. We were removing ones just like them, there at the Intervale, in order to make room for a new apple orchard. But Bonnie was inspired by the revelation that the trees could be tapped prior to being cut down. The syrup might be another thing that the Intervale could offer through their CSA shares, and thus another form of income for the always-struggling community farm. Like Tove Jansson addressing her distant friend, Eva, I felt like I had Sherry and Virgil there with me; their presence was conjured through the knowledge they had passed along to me back when we used to hang out. It made the company of strangers less strange and the hard work less hard.

The expression *take heart*, then, is really a call to take courage along with everything else that requires taking—time, risks, opportunities, and care. It's about discovering friendly spaces for failure and also about constructing them, working to expose the easier, softer side of what might look and feel hard to others. It's the end point, or final challenge, presented by these five cues about what it takes to hang out. The point, with each, is that the social musculature is already there. What is needed is merely the resolve to access and put it all to use. Time, risks, opportunities, care, and heart: five varieties of action that set the grand machinery of humanity into motion and, with a little effort, might just keep it all humming along.

AFTERWORD

HANGING OUT AS THE WATERS RISE

I recently spent an afternoon at the end of the world. It happened in Seattle: I was visiting my family there, just as I do most summers. My partner Dave was with me and so was my mother. She was clinging to my arm when the three of us stepped forward into a dark, mist-smeared void where the air around us smelled acrid and briny and suggestive of ruin.

For the first few minutes we just stood there, huddling near the threshold and close to the memory of light. It was all we could do while we waited for our eyes to adjust. Then, as they did, we started to explore the space around us. What we found were bodies, people. Some of them were standing, some of them were propped against the walls, and some were splayed out on the floor, corpse-like. We picked our ways around and over them at first. Then we joined them.

In a far corner, I got to my knees and helped my mother, who is in her seventies, into a sitting position. Then I stretched out on the floor as I had seen others doing and she and Dave did the same. We stared upward at a faint beam of light that was spattered with moving shadow. It would come and go, undulating, fading, and then surging forth before cutting out completely again. In the moments when it shone most brightly, I could see the others there in the room—there must have been twenty or thirty of them—but then they would disappear again and I would be left alone, or seemingly alone, in a quick privacy of darkness.

All the while, sound stalked the space. It grew from a deep swelling of bass that migrated in a rush throughout the room, filling it from end to end. Then came a storm of sonic texture: tearing, scratching, digging, shredding, burning. I could hear wild dogs rooting amongst debris and also nervous human whispers, barely audible. Finally, these sounds subsided and were replaced by a choir. It sang in an unknown language and moved haltingly from a series of minor chords to, at last, a major one, sounding a note of shy hope. Above the choir, a falsetto voice floated lightly, like sun on water.

The whole thing took about twenty-five minutes. Dave, my mother, and I stayed longer, though—enough to watch the whole cycle unfold multiple times. Others around us did, too, electing to bear witness to an end that seemed to have no end, that just kept coming. The first time through, I surprised myself by crying. The tears ran into my ears and my hair as I lay there on the floor, wedged between the bodies of two people I love. I cried over a simulated experience of profound and devastating loss. I had mislaid the world I knew: I was floating in space, I was buried under ground, I was cloistered in the hold of a ship and set adrift and rocking on waves.

Then, as the cycle started over once more, I gradually regained my awareness of my actual surroundings. I was in a room, a familiar one. I could feel the carpet beneath me. It hadn't been there a few Christmases ago when I'd visited the same room to view the works of a nineteenth-century Danish painter on display there. Back then, it had been polished hardwood to match the gleaming gilt frames of the paintings. Now it was darkness and smoke and bodies, including that of a man in a Seahawks jersey who was seated in a half-lotus position just across from me.

From my vantage point in the corner, I could watch others arrive and enter into our shared void. They would stumble in and stand there as I had stood there, struck dumb by the darkness which, for me, had grown less threatening and more familiar. Then, as the bass tones announced another cycle beginning, I helped my mother to her feet and collected her purse from the ground and the three of us wound back through the sea of bodies, toward the bright July day that waited for us outside.

The occasion for this sojourn to the end of the world was, in reality, an art exhibit called *FLÓÐ* by the Icelandic multimedia artist Jónsi, which was designed for site-specific presentation at the National Nordic Museum in Seattle. I didn't know it at the time, but I had actually experienced the whole thing in the wrong order. The combination of light, sound, and scented fog, as Jónsi explains in interviews, is actually supposed to begin with the hopeful choir part and end with the violent destruction part. What starts out as "16 voices distributed individually across speakers" becomes "a big wave"; the voices are drowned by the wave and then replaced by a mix of field recordings and "textures," as he calls them—all of it serving as a metaphor for rising seas brought about by climate change. Jónsi, who is also the lead singer of the melodic post-rock band Sigur Rós, says that the installation grew out of his own fixation on "the big wave and how we're all gonna die and everything is gonna flood."[1] The idea was to become engulfed, it seemed, not to emerge.

But that's not how I experienced it. Rather, because my entrance into the gallery had coincided with the initial moment of destruction, what was supposed to exist before came afterwards for me.

The voices of the choir rose out of Jónsi's frenzy of sonic "textures" instead of the other way around. Seen in this way, the exhibit spoke not only of despair but also of hope, struggle, and of something new spluttering to life. The fact that Jónsi devised the piece as a loop actually invites this kind of inverse reading: without the benefit of clear beginnings and endings, the viewer is forced to discover entrances and exits for herself and to craft her own version of a story that might fall somewhere between those poles. This was what we were all doing in there, the twenty or thirty of us who rested and cried and looked and heard and hung out inside the space of the *FLÓÐ* exhibit. We were devising stories from the disjointed wreckage of sensory experience, trying to make meaning from it all. We were doing it separately, in accordance with our own logic and guided by our own subjective impressions, but we were doing it together. We were giving ourselves over to an experience of collective undoing, of mass fragility.

I carried that feeling of mass fragility with me when I left the exhibit. It clung to me, a bit like how my mother had clung to my arm for balance when we were inside it. I thought about what it meant to have hung out, without conversation and with little shared acknowledgement, in that space of simulated disaster. I thought about the guy in the Seahawks jersey, about the cautious way that we eyed each other, saw each other. And because the exhibit encouraged me to, I compared my impressions of it to real disasters, both hypothetical and otherwise.

About three weeks before I'd left for Seattle, you see, my home state of Vermont had flooded. It all started with rain that fell and fell—two whole, uninterrupted days' worth of it. Even as I write this some months later, the flood and its aftermath is still very much with us in Vermont, though the rain did eventually stop. The public high school in Montpelier where I gather on Tuesday nights with other bagpipers—a precious experience when you play an eccentric instrument like the bagpipes—has only recently reopened its doors to us. Just a week ago, there were still FEMA trailers taking up space in its parking lot. Its ground floor was entirely submerged in the July floods. The same goes for much of Montpelier, which is the state's capital. It's downtown district has yet to regain a sense of normalcy and many of the businesses there are still closed. The bar where, the summer before, I sat and talked about hanging out and *Hanging Out* with a friend over some fries and lunch beers—the same bar where I had dinner with a long-lost college friend who I hadn't seen in fifteen years, but who showed up to a reading I was doing at a local library—is still closed. All over the state, the rivers and waterfalls where I delight in swimming each summer continue to run high, which has prevented me from going near them. The Intervale Community Farm where I do my volunteering, which saw 99% of its land submerged in the floods, had to temporarily halt its CSA program. The flower farm next door, where Dave and I danced on the grass at a concert back in June, amidst zinnias and black-eyed susans, is a welter of mud.

I talk a lot about space in *Hanging Out* because space is one of the essential ingredients required for social activity. In the wake of the Vermont floods, though, I was thinking not just about the scarcity of spaces that foster such activity but also about the constant vulnerability that defines them even when they manage to exist. The *FLÓÐ* exhibit in Seattle nudged all of this thinking one step further: it brought me face-to-face with the prospect—indeed, the virtual experience—of their total erasure.

Crisis can bring about a much-needed confrontation with community. It's not the best or most desirable way to hang out, obviously, but it's one way that hanging out happens. Rebecca Solnit, in a book she wrote on the subject of communities that form in the wake of crisis, observes as much, noting how "Disaster requires an ability to embrace contradiction in both the minds of those undergoing it and those trying to understand it from afar." One of the more fertile outgrowths of such contradiction is, as Solnit documents, camaraderie: disasters bring about profound disruptions to individual experience, but they also create new openings and spaces for the creation of extra-individual, or communal, catharsis. "In each disaster, there is suffering, there are psychic scars that will be felt most when the emergency is over, there are deaths and losses," Solnit writes, but there are also "satisfactions, newborn social bonds, and liberations."[2]

In Seattle, while lying on a carpet surrounded by the prostrate bodies of loved ones and strangers alike, I thought about hypothetical floods, future floods, and also about real floods. Back when I lived in North Dakota, for example, it was in a town where, some decades before I arrived, flooding had prompted the largest evacuation of an American population since the Civil War. On my regular runs through the downtown district, I would pass by the flood monument, which takes the form of a sandstone and concrete pillar rising beside the river that was once the cause of the town's suffering. It marks the high-water point from the 1997 disaster: 54.35 feet. I would pause at its base and look up and imagine the glint of light reaching toward me through all that water.

In October 2019, when coastal hurricanes pushed heavy rains inland and delivered them to the Midwest, Dave and I mucked our basement out with borrowed gear from neighbors. The whole street passed shop vacs around and helped to drag heavy rolls of water-logged carpet out of houses, piling them on berms alongside broken furniture and strips of muddy flooring. Then, again, in the spring of 2020, as the Covid pandemic descended, Dave and I found ourselves running monotonous figure eights through our North Dakota neighborhood because the river, having jumped its banks yet again, was blocking our usual running route. We couldn't trace our normal path to the old flood monument because we had a flood of our own to deal with.

I have lived with floods and also with their historical scars. I have walked streets that were born anew because of water and likewise those that were decimated by it, rinsed of the things—homes and businesses and parks and trees—that once made them so livable. And I have stood on bridges in the company of neighbors and friends and strangers alike and watched the water go thundering by. Annie Dillard, in her classic work *Pilgrim at Tinker Creek*, writes memorably about a similar experience that rocked her rural Virginia community. "Neighbors who have barely seen each other all winter are there, shaking their heads. Few have ever seen it before: the water is *over* the bridge," she writes, noting how the spectacle of rising water has drawn people out of their homes.[3] This is the thing about weather, which is also the thing about water: when it comes, it comes for everyone and thus creates ready-made forms of connection and instant topics of conversation. It shouldn't take a flood in order to hang out. But sometimes, that's exactly what it takes.

One of the things that came out of the 1997 flood in Grand Forks was the creation of a new town square. Decades later, it was in that town square that I first met my friend who became a reality

TV star. I attended town dances in that square as well as farmer's markets; I did yoga in that square as part of a town-wide wellness week; and though I do not ice skate, I watched ice skaters there each December when town officials flooded the square—on purpose this time—so it would freeze and form a rink.

The environmental literature scholar Christopher Schaberg, in his elegiac work *Searching for the Anthropocene*, writes about how water, in the context of climate change, becomes a bigger and more inevitable facet of life on earth. There is no choice but to notice the water that threatens to rise, or recede, or otherwise reshape the land around us.

> Part of the Anthropocene is realizing the inescapability of being on the water, in varying senses of that term. This means coastal erosion and melting icecaps as much as dying reefs and rogue tempests. It's how humans are comprised of and depend on water, to a limit. How we maintain awareness of this fact and consciously interact with water – or ignore it, or repress this reality—may be one of the crucial indicators of how the Anthropocene plays out.[4]

The term "Anthropocene" formalizes the link between human behavior and the natural world by naming a process of epochal transformation that left lasting impacts on the earth. It marks the dawn of human dominance over nature and also the entrenchment of certain social habits that took shape alongside that quest for dominance. Among those social habits is privacy, or the process by which human independence came to be seen as a good thing, a privileged thing, an honorable thing, instead of as the opposite of any of that. As the world has become more human—more subject to the whims of human-centered activity and more committed to carrying on in spite of the consequences—so too has it become more lonely.

Hanging out, then, becomes a means of processing those feelings of mass fragility and an antidote to the loneliness that would seek to weaponize and turn them against us. Rather than avoiding the messiness and complications of others, hanging out becomes a way of embracing it *and* them, of turning towards instead of away from the catastrophe that beckons, whether via rising floodwaters or forests set aflame. After all, it's easier to prepare when you can see what's coming.

I have done a lot of hanging out since the hardcover publication of *Hanging Out*. There have been interviews and podcast appearances and presentations and public readings. And from these interactions, I have acted as an audience to others' efforts to make hanging out happen—to their iron-clad determination to see that work done, in spite of all the complexities that are known or feared to come with it. This tendency is like a version of what Lauren Berlant calls "wanting the world," a desire which often meets with opposition in the form of "inconvenience." As Berlant writes, "The inconvenience of the world is at its most confusing when one wants the world but resists some of the costs of wanting."[5] All desire comes with a cost and where the world is concerned, those costs can be multitudinous and intimidating. But what Berlant gets at in *On the Inconvenience of Other People*, which was the last book they ever wrote, is how inconvenience is less of a fact than an invention. As such, it is only ever partially true. Its factualness lies chiefly in its inevitability: "*We cannot know each other without being inconvenient to each other,*" Berlant insists.[6] What this means is that to be in the world and of the world means to be with it, as well, and to bear all the burdens—grammatical and otherwise—that descend from that whole string of prepositions. Hanging out is a way to experience the *in* and the *of* and the *with* all at once, with an awareness of the mess that often results from doing so. It's a way to not just address the problems and stresses of that "mass fragility" that I have been talking about but to actively crowdsource solutions in order to construct a path that leads elsewhere, out of the clutches of mass fragility.

It's work that cannot be done cleanly or comfortably and work that cannot be carried out in isolation. This is what makes hanging out—which requires the suspension of minor forms of personal discomfort in the name of enhanced social connection—an essential part of that work. Hanging out is about more than improvisation and play, though it starts with both; it's about acknowledging the work that needs to be done and playing at it together.

So many of the conversations that I've been having since the initial publication of *Hanging Out* have occurred in the places that give rise to that sort of work. I'm talking about third places, of course: libraries, schools, bookstores, coffee shops, meeting halls, and even grocery stores (I was elated to see *Hanging Out* cited in, of all places, a local Vermont grocery store's weekly circular). But these places, though they fight against the incursion of those feelings of mass fragility, are not immune to its effects. If anything, they are extra vulnerable to them and thus liable to end up neglected or forgotten, until rising flood waters compel us to remember how much we actually need them. It shouldn't take a flood in order to hang out, or to remind us of how much we depend on the places and people and institutions that endure for the sake of allowing us to hang out. It shouldn't because, if it does, then it might already be too late.

The German-born philosopher Hannah Arendt, writing about her adopted home country in the 1940s, observes that people in America are lonely because they are busy. "In this country," she tells her friend Gershom Scholem, "one gets very lonely because people have so many things to do that, after a certain point, the need for leisure is quite simply no longer there. The result of this is a certain absence (by which I mean absent-mindedness) that makes the contact between people so difficult."[7] Arendt's point is that the strain brought about by constant activity, or by the apparent necessity of performing such activity, prevents one from not just enjoying but even experiencing leisure. Labor becomes the guiding mantra lurking behind all experience, regardless of the particular objective, and hanging out—what Arendt calls "the contact between people"—starts to feel unmanageable. Similarly, the media scholar Marshall Berman, writing decades ago in the 1980s, described the conditions of modernity as precarious, frenetic, and seemingly prone to evaporation. In his classic book *All That Is Solid Melts Into Air* comments on the paradox of unity, which he calls "a unity of disunity."[8] Modernity, Berman says, refers to a set of circumstances that everyone on earth is fated to experience; its power lies, ironically enough, in convincing them that they are the first to experience them, and in thus making them feel helpless and alone. All that is believed to be solid, then, melts into air—it dissipates on the wind and becomes impossible to catch.

In our present moment, we find a situation that is at once quite similar to Berman's (and Arendt's too, for that matter) and yet also more advanced. All that is firm dissolves into liquid. It ends up in the sea, or in the nearest river, or it slips through our fingers and disappears down the drain. This is how it feels to watch the waters rise, and this is also why it feels so hard to hang out sometimes. There is a liquidness to contemporary life, a feeling that one is caught up in the current of things that must get done yet never seem to make anything better, to recall Arendt. Hanging out means acquiring the capacity and the will to stand still and let the water go rushing past, if even for a moment. It means calling the friend you've been meaning to call, striking up a conversation with a stranger, getting to know your neighbor, volunteering, or joining a club or committee.

In order to tackle the big existential threats of our time, we have to be alive to the opportunities that can come to us through the work of treading water, of standing still, of hanging out. I'm not proposing hanging out as an antidote to the manifold problems of climate change. But I am saying that hanging out, which involves pausing to take stock of one's position within a vast web of social ties, might form the foundation of activities that help to unravel the knot of economic, environmental, and social challenges that *is* climate change.

Now is the time to hang out. So was yesterday. But tomorrow will also do, in a pinch.

ACKNOWLEDGMENTS

A book is a polyvocal thing and this one is filled with the voices of those who have helped me write it. That includes Paul Devlin, David Hering, Robert Kilpatrick, and Mike Miley, who read chapter drafts and offered encouragement along with commentary. It also includes those friends and colleagues of mine who appear throughout the book, and whose stories and experiences rubbed up against, or merged with, my own: thanks to Virgil Benoit, Joe Egar, Ronny Ewanek, Carleton Gholz, Nick Hagen, Kacie Harold, Tom Hoffman, Amy Kielmeyer, E. M. Miller Saunders, Sherry O'Donnell, Michelle Rydz, Rob Snyder, Paul Sum, and Molly Yeh, along with, no doubt, many more. The same goes for the former members of The Armadillos (Austin, Matt, and Josh) and Callán (Kip, Cara, Steve, and Steve), along with the members of Smokestack Lightning (Nick, Phil, William, Dave, Steve, and Heidi), and my regular Cascade

Mountains backpacking compatriots (Stu, Andy, Mac, Isabella, Ian, Jeff, John, and Candace).

In lieu of institutional acknowledgments, I'd like to mention that this book was written without the support of any grants, fellowships, sabbatical periods, course releases, or research assistance. It was, however, completed with the generous, informal support of many wonderful colleagues and students. Thanks, especially, to the members of my WRT 337 Advanced Creative Nonfiction class, held during the Spring 2022 semester at Champlain College, and to my colleagues Ryan Ruby, Jonathan Beecher Field, and Jen Rose Smith, for being down to hang out and talk about hanging out. And thank you to my friends and associates on Twitter, and to everyone who contributes to making social media spaces like it more, as opposed to less, supportive and sustaining.

I struck intellectual and editorial gold when I met Mike Lindgren. My thanks to him, for his enthusiasm and guidance, and to everyone else at Melville House.

My final thanks are to my family: to my parents, Jim and Sandra Liming; to my sister, Faye; to my brother-in-law, Daniel; and to my partner, Dave. I love hanging out with the whole lot of you.

NOTES

INTRODUCTION

1   Christopher Ingraham, "Every County in America, Ranked by Scenery and Climate," *The Washington Post*, August 17, 2015, https://www.washingtonpost.com/news/wonk/wp/2015/08/17/every-county-in-america-ranked-by-natural-beauty/.

2   Amelia Horgan, *Lost in Work: Escaping Capitalism* (London: Pluto Books, 2021), 84.

3   Antonio Gramsci, *Letters from Prison* (New York: Columbia University Press, 2011), 134.

4   Jenny Odell, *How to Do Nothing: Resisting the Attention Economy* (Brooklyn: Melville House, 2019), xvii.

5   Rebecca Solnit, *Wanderlust: A History of Walking* (New York: Penguin, 2000), 10.

6   Vivek H. Murthy, *Together: The Healing Power of Connection in a Sometimes Lonely World* (New York: Harper Wave, 2020), 37.

7   Ibid., 38.

8   Zadie Smith, *Intimations: Six Essays* (New York: Penguin, 2020), 21.

1. HANGING OUT AT PARTIES

1 Raymond Williams, *Keywords: A Vocabulary of Culture and Society* (Oxford: Oxford University Press, 1976), 9.
2 Ibid.
3 Ibid., 13.
4 Ibid., 14.
5 *The Compact Edition of the Oxford English Dictionary* (Oxford: Oxford University Press, 1971), 514.
6 Thomas Starkey, *A Dialogue Between Pole and Lupset* (London: Royal Historical Society, 1989 [1538]), 65.
7 *The Compact Edition of the Oxford English Dictionary*, 515.
8 Madame de Gomez, *La Belle Assemblée*, tr. Eliza Haywood (London: D. Browne, 1743), 192. Available online: Hathitrust.org, https://catalog. hathitrust.org/Record/008979344.
9 Ibid.
10 Carson McCullers, *The Heart Is a Lonely Hunter* (New York: Mariner Books, 2000 [1940]), 102.
11 Ibid., 105.
12 Ibid., 113.
13 Ibid., 115.
14 Henry Green, *Party Going*, from *Loving—Living—Party Going* (New York: Penguin, 1993 [1939]), 396.
15 Raymond Williams, "Structures of Feeling," from *Marxism and Literature* (Oxford: Oxford University Press, 1977), 132.
16 Green, 424.
17 Virginia Woolf, *Mrs. Dalloway* (New York: Harcourt, 1981 [1925]), 122.
18 McCullers, 116.
19 Audre Lorde, "The Electric Slide Boogie," from *The Collected Poems of Audre Lorde* (New York: W. W. Norton, 1997), 474.
20 Ibid.
21 Woolf, *Mrs. Dalloway*, 122.

2. HANGING OUT WITH STRANGERS

1 *Victoria*, dir. Sebastian Schipper (Senator Film, 2015).
2 Walter Benjamin, *The Arcades Project* (Cambridge: Harvard University Press, 2002), 517.
3 Ibid., 517–520.
4 Rick Moody, *Hotels of North America* (Boston: Little, Brown and Company, 2015), 170.
5 Lauren Berlant, *Desire / Love* (Santa Barbara: Punctum Books, 2012), 53.
6 Irvine Welsh, *Trainspotting* (New York: W. W. Norton, 1996), 263.
7 Ibid., 264.

8   Ibid., 308.
9   Robert Walser, *Berlin Stories* (New York: NYRB Classics, 2012), 9.
10   Ibid., 89.

3. JAMMING AS HANGING OUT

1   Hayden Carruth, "The Main Thing about Improvisation," in *Sitting In: Selected Writings on Jazz, Blues, and Related Topics* (Iowa City: University of Iowa Press, 1986), 99.
2   Carruth, "The Guy Downstairs," in *Sitting In*, 1.
3   Ibid., 2.
4   Amit Chaudhuri, *Finding the Raga* (New York: New York Review Books, 2021), 154.
5   Derek Bailey, *Improvisation: Its Nature and Practice in Music* (New York: Da Capo, 1992), xii.
6   Dan DiPiero, *Contingent Encounters: Improvisation in Music and Everyday Life* (Ann Arbor, MI: University of Michigan Press, 2022), 2.
7   Fred Moten, *In the Break: The Aesthetics of the Black Radical Tradition* (Minneapolis: University of Minnesota Press, 2003), 63.
8   James Baldwin, "Sonny's Blues," in *The Norton Introduction to Literature, Shorter 13th Edition*, ed. Kelly Mays (New York: W. W. Norton, 2019), 102.
9   Ibid.
10   Ibid., 112.
11   Ibid., 113.
12   Stefano Harney and Fred Moten, *The Undercommons: Fugitive Planning and Black Study* (New York: Minor Compositions, 2013), 110.
13   Carruth, "The Guy Downstairs," 9.

4. HANGING OUT ON TV

1   Sigmund Freud, "The 'Uncanny,'" in *Writings on Art and Literature*, ed. James Strachey (Redwood City, CA: Stanford University Press, 1997), 195.
2   Mark Greif, *Against Everything* (New York: Pantheon, 2016), 177.
3   Ibid.
4   Andrew O'Hehir, in David Shields, *Reality Hunger: A Manifesto* (New York: Knopf, 2010), 82.
5   Shields, *Reality Hunger*, 5.
6   Freud, "The 'Uncanny,'" 212.
7   Greif, *Against Everything*, 180.
8   *My People Are My Home* (Twin City Women's Film Collective, 1976).
9   Meridel Le Sueur, *Crusaders* (New York: Blue Heron Press, 1955), https://www.loc.gov/resource/lhbum.13869/.
10   *My People Are My Home*.

5. HANGING OUT ON THE JOB

1   "Data Snapshot: Contingent Faculty in U.S. Higher Ed," *AAUP Updates*, October 11, 2018, American Association of University Professors, https://www.aaup.org/news/data-snapshot-contingent-faculty-us-higher-ed#.Yr3mDpDMLep.

2   Tom McCarthy, *Satin Island* (New York: Knopf, 2015), 110.

3   Ibid., 101.

4   Ibid., 119.

5   Ibid., 14

6   Ibid., 20.

7   Ray Oldenburg, "Our Vanishing Third Places," *Planning Commissioners Journal*, no. 25 (Winter 1996–1997): 5, https://j6p3d5c7.stackpathcdn.com/wp-content/uploads/1997/01/184.pdf.

8   Ibid., 7.

9   Ray Oldenburg, *The Great Good Place* (Philadelphia: Da Capo Press, 1999), 11.

10   Walter Benjamin, *The Arcades Project* (Cambridge: Harvard University Press, 1999), 216.

11   Oscar Wilde, "The Decay of Lying," in *Intentions* (1889; Project Gutenberg, April 24, 1997).

12   Benjamin, *The Arcades Project*, 221.

13   Theodor Adorno, "Antithesis," in *Minima Moralia* (New York: Verso, 2005), 26.

6. DINNER PARTIES AS HANGING OUT

1   Ralph Waldo Emerson, "Friendship," in *Essays* (Cambridge, MA: Riverside Press, 1865), 189.

2   M.F.K. Fisher, *Serve It Forth* (New York: North Point Press, 1937), 114.

3   Ibid., 115.

4   M.F.K. Fisher, *How to Cook a Wolf* (New York: North Point Press, 1942), 192.

5   "Stacey Abrams's Dream Dinner Party," *Bon Appétit*, June 2021, 88.

6   "Julian Fellowes's Dream Dinner Party," *Bon Appétit*, March 2022, 88.

7   Fisher, *Serve It Forth*, 48.

8   John Stuart Mill, *Principles of Political Economy*, ed. J. Laurence Laughlin (New York: Appleton, 1885; Project Gutenberg, September 27, 2009), 105, https://www.gutenberg.org/ebooks/30107.

9   *Next Floor*, dir. Denis Villeneuve, written by Jacques Davidts and Phoebe Greenberg (Phi, 2008), https://www.youtube.com/watch?v=t60MMJH_1ds.

10   Industrial Workers of the World, "Pyramid of Capitalist System" (Cleveland, OH: The International Publishing Company, 1911). Available online: https://commons.wikimedia.org/wiki/File:Anti-capitalism_color.jpg

11   Associated Press, "North Dakota University Chancellor Denies Harassment Claims," *Diverse Issues in Higher Education*, November 17, 2017, https://www.diverseeducation.com/news-roundup/article/15101691/north-dakota-university-chancellor-denies-harassment-claims.

12   Seneca, quoted in Fisher, *Serve It Forth*, 46.

13   Fisher, *Serve It Forth*, 13.

14   Kim Stanley Robinson, "Sacred Space," in *I'm With the Bears: Short Stories from a Damaged Planet* (New York: Verso, 2011), 74.

7. HANGING OUT ON THE INTERNET

1   Wallace Stegner, *Wolf Willow: A History, a Story, and a Memory of the Last Plains Frontier* (New York: Penguin, 2000), 8.

2   Calvin Kasulke, *Several People Are Typing* (New York: Doubleday, 2021), 121.

3   Ibid., 93.

4   Immanuel Kant, *Critique of Judgment*, in *The Norton Anthology of Theory and Criticism* (1790; New York: Norton, 2018), 446.

5   Ibid., 449.

6   Ibid., 451.

7   Kasulke, *Several People Are Typing*, 80.

8   Michael Witmore, "Adjacencies, Virtuous and Vicious, and the Forking Paths of Library Research," *Wine Dark Sea*, July 8, 2014, http://winedarksea.org/?p=1942.

9   Daniel Rosenberg, "Stop, Words," *Representations* 127, no. 1 (Summer 2014), 84.

10   Ibid., 85.

11   Tove Jansson, *Letters from Tove*, ed. Boel Westin and Helen Svensson, trans. Sarah Death (Minneapolis: University of Minnesota Press, 2020), 104.

12   Ibid., 113.

13   Ibid., 131.

14   Ibid., 134.

15   Ibid., 191.

16   Kant, *Critique of Judgment*, 453.

CONCLUSION: HOW TO HANG OUT

1   Yves Citton, *The Ecology of Attention*, trans. Barnaby Norman (New York: Polity, 2017), 3; emphasis original.

2   "About," Lex, accessed July 25, 2022, https://thisislex.app/.

3   Derek Thompson, "This Is What Happens When There Are Too Many Meetings," *The Atlantic*, April 4, 2022 https://www.theatlantic.com/newsletters/archive/2022/04/triple-peak-day-work-from-home/629457/.

4   Theodor Adorno, "Free Time," in *The Culture Industry: Selected Essays on*

Mass Culture (New York: Routledge, 2001), 188.

5   Jenny Odell, *How to Do Nothing: Resisting the Attention Economy* (Brooklyn: Melville House, 2019), xviii.

6   Octavia E. Butler, "Furor Scribendi," in *Bloodchild and Other Stories* (New York: Seven Stories Press, 2005), 140.

7   Virginia Woolf, *To the Lighthouse* (New York: Harvest Books, 1981), 161.

8   Theodor Adorno, "The Culture Industry Reconsidered," in *The Culture Industry: Selected Essays on Mass Culture* (New York: Routledge, 2001), 100.

AFTERWORD: HANGING OUT AS THE WATERS RISE

1   Jónsi, quoted in Jas Keimig "The Flood is Coming," *The Stranger*, 16 March 2023.

2   Rebecca Solnit, "A Paradise Built in Hell" (excerpt), *The New York Times*, 20 August 2009.

3   Annie Dillard, *Pilgrim at Tinker Creek* (Harper Perennial Classics, 1998), 153.

4   Christopher Schaberg, *Searching for the Anthropocene* (Bloomsbury, 2022), 45-6.

5   Lauren Berlant, *On the Inconvenience of Other People* (Duke University Press, 2022), 9.

6   Ibid., 7.

7   Hannah Arendt, *The Correspondence of Hannah Arendt and Gershom Scholem*, ed. Marie Luise Knott, trans. Anthony David (University of Chicago Press, 2017), 18.

8   Marshall Berman, *All That Is Solid Melts Into Air: The Experience of Modernity* (Penguin Books, 1981), 15.

INDEX

SHEILA LIMING is an associate professor at Champlain College in Burlington, Vermont, and the author of two previous books, *What a Library Means to a Woman* and *Office*. She has been featured in the *New York Times* Arts & Leisure section as well in periodicals ranging from *People* magazine to *Bookforum* and *Slate*. She has been a guest on the Ezra Klein show and on numerous NPR programs, as well as on KCBS San Francisco and WDET Detroit. Her essays have appeared in venues like *The Atlantic, McSweeney's, Lapham's Quarterly, The Los Angeles Review of Books, Public Books,* and *The Point*.